Basic
Printmaking
Techniques

Joan Miró, One illustration from the book A Toute Epreuve (2 vols., 80 color woodcuts). Courtesy Museum of Fine Arts, Boston. Seth K. Sweetser Fund.

Basic Printmaking Techniques

Bernard Toale

Davis Publications, Inc.
Worcester, Massachusetts

Acknowledgments:

A book is always the product of many people's efforts. The artists that I have included have inspired me. Without their innovations there would be no need for me to document the growth of the techniques I've covered. To all of them I am extremely grateful.

I am also grateful for the generosity extended toward me by print publishers and galleries around the country. They include: Tyler Graphics Ltd.; Shark's Inc.; Smith Anderson Editions; William Greenbaum Fine Prints; Dolan/Maxwell Gallery; Solo Editions; Pace Editions; Grenfell Press; The Akin Gallery; Diane Villani Editions; Peter Blum Editions; The Alpha Gallery; Mary Ryan Gallery; Mulberry Press; Cone Editions Press; The Graphics Workshop; Stewart and Stewart; Damage Press; Houston Fine Arts; Vinal Haven Press; and, Preston Graphics.

Kay Canavino documented all of the process sequences and learned more about printmaking than she ever wanted to, and my oldest friend in the world, Leo Abbett, did the illustrations once again. Roger Rodriguez was a real big help.

Wyatt Wade and Martha Siegel deserve merit awards for perseverance and courtesy in coaxing me along. I am also grateful to Joe Zina for not giving me too much of a hard time.

I hope you'll enjoy and use this book.

Front cover: Terence La Noue, *Tarantella Series I,* 1988. Monotype, collage, hand-colored, 55 ¾ x 76 ¼" (142 x 194 cm). Printed and published by Tyler Graphics Ltd. Copyright Terence La Noue/Tyler Graphics Ltd., 1988.

Back cover: Gregory Amenoff, *Untitled,* 1989. Woodcut, ten blocks, sixteen colors; 54 x 48" (137 x 122 cm). Courtesy Houston Fine Art Press.

Printed in Mexico
Library of Congress Catalog Card Number: 91-073903
ISBN: 87192-237-1

Interior Design and Composition: Greta D. Sibley

10 9 8 7 6

preface

ABOUT THIS BOOK

I have chosen to focus in this book on the three techniques that I know the best and that I have found to complement each other when used in the classroom and the artist's studio. Relief prints, monotypes and silkscreen prints can all be done with a minimal amount of training and equipment. They can be learned quickly.

The print is sought after in today's art market. Relief prints carry with them a long tradition and a generally recognizable style filled with vibrato and emotion. The simplicity of the monotype process is a great introduction to those who may shun printmaking because they fear that it is too technical. Silkscreen is a good vehicle to introduce students and artists to photographic processes and the satisfactions of working with broad, flat areas of color. And it can

At the Tyler Graphics studios, larger scale print plates often require several people to ink them.

Several people may also be required for printing. Photographs courtesy Tyler Graphics Ltd.

be used in combination with relief and monotype processes to create prints of great power and complexity.

It is my hope that this book will get you started in printmaking. I've tried to fill it with images made today. This is what you'll see when you go into museums and galleries exhibiting fine prints. I hope they will excite you. I hope they will annoy you. I hope they will inspire you to do it yourself and to invent other ways. Art teaches us about ourselves. I hope this book will give you a few tools to speed that process along.

*Frank Stella, **La Penna di Hu** (Black and White), 1988. Relief, etching and aquatint, 77 ½ x 58 ¾" (197 x 149 cm), edition of 42. Courtesy Tyler Graphics Ltd. Copyright Frank Stella/Tyler Graphics Ltd., 1988. Photo: Steven Sloman.*

contents

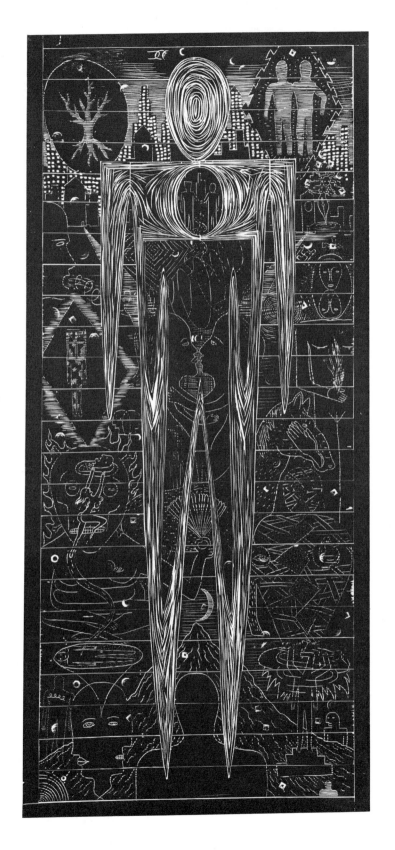

*John Buck, **Father and Son**, 1986.*
Color woodcut, 82 ½ x 36 ½"
(210 x 93 cm), edition of 30.
Courtesy Shark's Inc.

introduction

1

The history of humanity is a time line of communication. Sound first allowed people to share their fears and beliefs. Much later, the printed image — given great impetus by the invention of papermaking techniques — helped spread these beliefs to others. As the world has grown, so has the need for more and brighter and bigger visual symbols. Artists have responded, technologies have developed, and today we live in a world where a Fax machine sends the printed word around the globe by telephone, and Coke's familiar red and white logo is printed everywhere you look.

Communication is a basic human need. And from this need the art of printmaking was born.

In the beginning, printmaking was a way to make simple copies. It took images of our idols and spread

*Emil Nolde, **Storm**, 1906. Woodcut on dark cream laid paper, 6 ¼ x 7 ⅜"
(16 x 19 cm). Courtesy Museum of Fine Arts, Boston.*

Paul Gauguin, **Eve.** *Woodcut. Courtesy Museum of Fine Arts, Boston. Bequest of W. G. Russell Allen.*

them. It put our laws into tangible form. At a certain point, however, it also took on a life of its own. It asserted its unique character into the world of art-making processes and became art itself. Today fine art printmaking has little to do with making simple copies or with spreading images to the masses. It has become a rarefied world of collaborative studios and publishers' deadlines. Small, expensive editions are produced by combining print techniques, papermaking, computer-generated imagery and almost anything the new technologies can provide. And these new, compelling images will inspire others, as history has shown us before.

MAJOR PRINTMAKING TECHNIQUES

Relief

Of all the forms of printmaking, the relief print is the most ancient. A new baby's inked fingerprint pressed on paper tells the story completely. The high spots catch the ink and whatever they touch carries the message. Wood and linoleum blocks are carved to remove areas of the image

*Designing for printmaking involves thinking in reverse. What appears on the left side of the printing plate will show up on the right side of the print. This detail of Frank Stella's **Swan Engraving III** is shown next to a section of the printmaking plate. Courtesy Tyler Graphics Ltd. Photo: Steven Sloman.*

that will remain uninked. Wood engravers refine the process, carving delicate lines that appear white when the image is printed. Collagraphs are collages onto which you roll ink to pick up the image of their textured surface. With all of these processes, paper is pressed against the inked block or plate to transfer the image. Sometimes this is the gentle pressure of a finger or a spoon on the back of a thin Oriental paper to enhance a shadowed area. At other times it might be tons of hydraulic pressure against a thick paper to get the proper embossing of a dimensional image. Whatever the approach, the relief print process offers a directness and simplicity that has made itself vital to artists for centuries.

Intaglio

Intaglio (pronounced "in-TAHL-ee-oh") printmaking is virtually the reverse of relief printmaking. You cut lines into the surface of the printmaking plate with a sharp tool or with acids. These recessed areas are filled with ink and the top surface is wiped clean. The pressure of the printing press forces paper against this plate. A positive image is created from the ink-filled lines. Intaglio printing affects the surface of the paper, leaving a characteristic embossing. Intaglio techniques include etching, engraving, drypoint, mezzotint and aquatint. Intaglio printmaking as a rule requires the use of a press and thicker paper for successful images. It was not until the fifteenth century that paper technology in Europe advanced to the point of having these sheets readily available to artists. It was then that intaglio processes really developed.

Lithography

This third major printmaking process, also called planographic printing, relies on a chemical reaction and a smooth printmaking plate. In this process, you draw directly on the printmaking plate with greasy crayons. The areas of the plate free of crayon marks are chemically treated to repel ink while the greasy areas attract it. Printing is done under the pressure of a lithographic press. The print has a smooth surface without embossed lines. Lithography developed in Germany in the late 1790s and it quickly grew to be the major graphics technique of the nineteenth and twentieth centuries.

Silkscreen

The most common stencil printing technique is silkscreen, or serigraphic printing, used extensively in textile decoration, in industry, and in fine art printmaking. With this process, you draw or mask out an image on a fine grade mesh fabric that is stretched on a framework. This frame rests just above the paper or cloth you will be printing on. Ink is pulled across the mesh and forced through it with a flat blade known as a squeegee. Sharp photographic images can be adhered to the screen to produce an exact copy of complicated imagery. This process is used widely in industry and as a fine art

technique. It was brought to new heights during the 1970s by artists Robert Rauschenberg and Andy Warhol and by the minimal art movement. It allowed these artists to create broad, flat areas of textureless color and to use photographic images on a large scale. Many silkscreen images were printed directly on canvas and displayed, as the artist intended, as one-of-a-kind paintings. Screened images are now used in combination with other painting techniques as a way to create specific detail in a unique image.

Monotype

A printing process which uses printmaking supplies but is incapable of producing multiple images is monotype. Monotypes have become increasingly popular with contemporary artists. They can be quick to produce and you don't need to learn complicated techniques. They also give unexpected results which can lead you to new ways of thinking about your work. You create a drawing on glass, Plexiglas or any smooth surface with ink, watercolor or oil paint. The drawing is covered with printing paper and either run through a press or rubbed by hand. After the image is transferred to the paper and the print is removed, some of the ink remains on the plate. This allows the artist to go back and rework the plate to create new variations of the image. Because the approach is similar to other printmaking processes, it is often a good way to introduce the idea of printmaking to artists who are not interested in technique.

Fingerprints reveal the essence of relief printmaking: raised surfaces hold the ink, while depressions remain free of ink and appear as white lines on the paper.

MAJOR PRINTMAKING TECHNIQUES

MONOTYPE: *Todd McKie,* **Small World***, 1989 (detail).*
16 x 20" (41 x 51 cm). Courtesy the artist.

RELIEF: *Judy McKie,* **Black Leopard***, 1990 (detail).*
Linocut, 24 x 18" (61 x 46 cm). Courtesy the artist.

RELIEF: *Judy McKie,* **Four Birds***, 1990 (detail).*
Woodcut, 23 x 20" (58 x 51 cm). Courtesy the artist.

RELIEF: *Beth Krommes,* **Peace on Earth***, 1989 (detail).*
Wood engraving, 5 x 4" (13 x 10 cm), edition of 200.
Courtesy the artist.

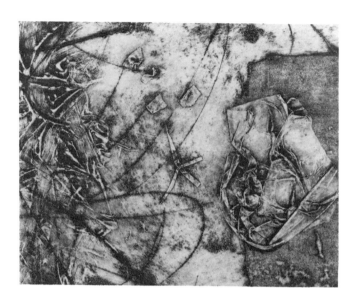

RELIEF: *Student work (detail). Collagraph, 6 x 9"
(15 x 23 cm).*

SILKSCREEN: *Leo Byrnes,* **The Rain Forest —
Endangered***, 1988 (detail). 26 x 21" (66 x 53 cm).*

INTAGLIO: *Richard Jacobs,* **Travelers***, 1990 (detail).
Etching, 31 x 23" (79 x 58 cm).*

LITHOGRAPHY: *Margie Hughto,* **Untitled***, 1987
(detail). 33 x 23" (84 x 58 cm).*

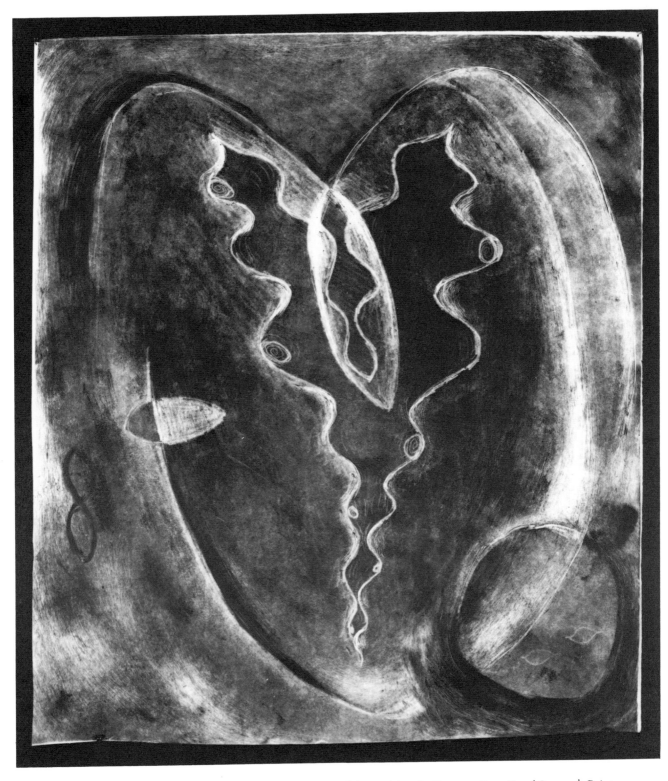

*Barbara Grad, **Spirit Song #6**, 1989. Monotype, 19 ¾ x 17 ½" (50 x 44 cm). Courtesy Rugg Road Paper & Prints.*

monotypes

monotypes

2

Monotypes are a great way to introduce artists and students to printmaking. A monotype is a painting or drawing done on a smooth surface such as Plexiglas, glass or metal etching plates. You transfer this image to another surface, usually paper or cloth, either with a printmaking press or with the pressure of a hand tool. Most of the ink is printed on the new surface. But a residue of ink and a ghost of the image remains on the printing plate. There are no carved lines in the printing plate as there are with etchings, linoleum and woodblock prints. Consequently no other exact image can be produced from this drawing. But the residual image left by the ink offers the artist a unique opportunity to create variations of this idea. This is one of the unique and exciting aspects of this process.

*Barbara Schwartz, **Untitled**, 1989. Monotype, 23 ½ x 26 ½"*
(60 x 67 cm). Courtesy Rugg Road Paper & Prints.

*Barbara Schwartz, **Untitled**, 1989. Monotype, 26 ½ x 20 ½" (67 x 52 cm). Courtesy Rugg Road Paper & Prints.*

The spontaneity of monotypes makes them the perfect medium for artists, students and teachers who love to experiment. The process is also inviting because it does not involve a lot of techniques. If you have ink, a surface to put it on, and paper, you can start making monotypes. Although the creation of monotypes is similar to painting and drawing, the transfer process allows you to create images and effects that you would not be able to achieve in any other way. Once you have printed one image, you can refer to and change the remnants of the image on the printing plate. You can make generation after generation of images informed by the ones that came before them. The speed of the process allows you to trace your thinking as you work and to move through many ideas in a short time.

One of the first artists to incorporate monotypes into his daily repertoire of techniques was a seventeenth century Italian painter named Giovanni Benedetto Castiglione. It is said that he invented the process around 1635 while working with etching, and many of his works resemble his etchings of that time. The techniques he developed then were simple and direct and are the same ones used by artists today.

Castiglione's first technique was simply to paint his image directly onto an etching plate and print it. The second was to cover the printing plate with a layer of ink and then scratch through it to make lines that would then appear white when printed. The third was a combination of these two, painting in some areas and scratching through in others.

Contemporary artists should realize that from the beginning this technique was used to enrich other areas of an artist's work. Because of its spontaneity, Castiglione could print quick sketches as studies for his etchings. The eighteenth century English artist William Blake chose other ways of making the process suit his needs. He toned areas in his etchings and used monotype as a way to create special effects in his oil and watercolor paintings. He often printed general areas of color in monotype and then worked over the inked image with other materials.

During the late 1800s a new interest in monotypes developed in Europe and the United States. A

Boston artist, Charles A. Walker, is credited with giving the process its name. He made several hundred monotypes. In France, the well-known painters of the day — Lautrec, Degas, Pissarro, Renoir, Gauguin and Cassatt — also tried their hands at this new technique. Degas made over 500 monotypes, both in their pure form and as underpaintings for his pastel drawings. Gauguin experimented extensively with monotypes and altered the process. By drawing on the back of the printing paper as it lay on the inked plate, he created a uniquely textured line. Matisse created a now famous series of portraits and figure drawings by inking the printing plate black and then removing ink with a stylus to create white lines. Monotype clubs formed in the early 1900s in New York and the process was finally given its place among the other art media.

Interest in monotypes today is greater than ever. Artists from all disciplines use it in its pure form or combine it with other processes. This experimentation continues to make it the most lively of the printmaking techniques.

*Joel Janowitz, **Untitled 11**, 1988. Monotype, 15 ½ x 19 ½" (39 x 50 cm). Courtesy Rugg Road Papers & Prints.*

WORKING SURFACE

The working surface for monotype can be almost anything smooth that will accept ink. Etching plates of copper or zinc can be used, but a more common surface is Plexiglas cut to the size of your image and then beveled. Beveling the plate prevents the paper from wrinkling as it runs through the press. One of the advantages of a clear plate is that you can put a sketch of your image underneath it for reference. Plexiglas is also lighter in weight than etching plates, and so allows you to work larger with less effort. You can create a more textured image by using linoleum, masonite, cardboard or thin plywood as your printing surface. Images can also be made on other paper and then transferred by printing from this "paper plate" onto your printing paper. The print will reflect some quality of whichever surface you choose.

TOOLS AND EQUIPMENT

A monotypist's tools are whatever suits his or her type of image. If you are doing a monotype with a dark background, rubber brayers or rollers can be used to cover the plate with ink. Sticks of varying thick-nesses, the handles of paintbrushes, Q-tips, rags, tarlatan (a stiff cheese-cloth used to wipe etchings) or any appropriate-sized object can be used to remove ink from the plate. Sol-vents can be applied to thin areas of ink to create tonal changes and tex-ture. With light ground monotypes, almost anything can be used to apply the ink to the plate. A brush, sponge, textured objects or your own gloved fingers will make marks

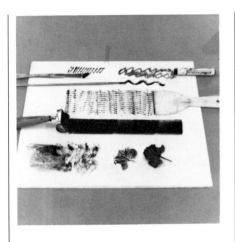

Ink can be applied to a monotype plate using a wide variety of implements and techniques.

Ink should be removed from the can evenly, leaving a flat surface of remaining ink. A paper skin is placed over the ink before closing the can. This skin will keep the ink from drying in the container.

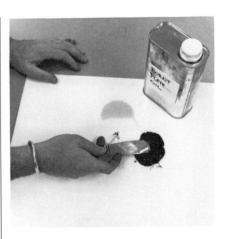

Additional burnt plate oil is often mixed with the ink to make it more fluid.

Rolling the ink on a Plexiglas plate from two directions will give you uniform coverage.

that will transfer and create unique printed images.

Certain types of monotype images and techniques require no printmaking press to print them. One of these is called a trace monotype. With this process, you lay paper on an inked plate and draw on the back of the paper with a stiff tool. The subtle pressure of the tool in combination with the artist's touch create tonal effects that can only be achieved without mechanical pressure. Hand rubbing a plate with a baren or a smooth object such as a large spoon or rounded stone, in combination with thin, Oriental-style paper, can result in beautiful prints with a wide range of tonalities in both light and dark field techniques.

A trace monotype can be made by placing a sheet of thin paper on the inked plate and drawing on the back of it.

Pressure from the drawing tool will cause the ink to transfer onto the paper.

A new sheet of paper can be placed on the same plate and rubbed with a baren.

This will pick up the negative image of the first print.

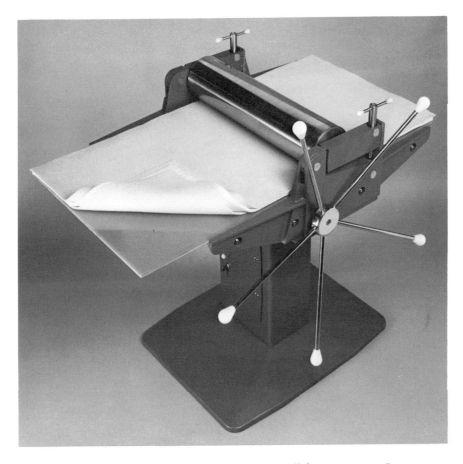

The KB Press was designed for etching and works well for monotypes. Courtesy KB Press, Hayward, CA.

The author's American French Tool Press can produce prints up to 40 x 60" (102 x 152 cm).

A printmaking press should be used with heavier European-style papers and dense printmaking inks. Slow, constant pressure is needed to pick up subtle washes of color and thin line drawings. A press also speeds up the printing process. Etching presses are the most common and versatile, and are used for linoleum and woodblock printing as well. Monotypes can also be printed on lithography and bookbinding presses. They all give slow, constant pressure on the plate and paper.

This Conrad press has several gear settings. This feature makes it versatile for wood, linoleum and monotypes which require slow, even, moderate pressure and for etchings which require heavy pressure. Courtesy Conrad Machine Company, Whitehall, Michigan.

The press should have three felts of different thicknesses. One lies on the printing paper and absorbs excess sizing as the print is rolled through the press. The second acts as a thick cushion to give even pressure to the print and to protect the press from the sharp edges of the plate. The third protects the first two from dirt and ink and stretches as the print is rolled through. This stretching protects the plate and image from distortion due to the rolling action of the press.

This school-grade press is well-suited for relief printmaking. Courtesy Hunt Manufacturing Company, Philadelphia, PA.

*This is an example of a trace monotype and a print made from the negative plate. Barbara Grad, **Spirit Song #20, 21**, 1989. Monotype and trace monotype, each 29 x 25" (74 x 64 cm). Courtesy Rugg Road Paper & Prints.*

INKS

Water-based inks

Beautiful effects can be achieved with water-based media. Their translucent qualities suit them to subtle uses of color, so they are best used with the additive process of direct painting. Water-based inks are particularly appropriate in classroom situations, where ventilation and safety concerns are more difficult to control and where easy cleanup is an advantage. There are now several good brands of water-based inks on the market.

On smooth, non-absorbent surfaces, water-based inks, gouache and watercolor have a tendency to "bead up" or refuse to stay where you put them. This can be overcome by adding a small amount of liquid dishwashing soap to the colorant. The soap will give the ink more body and reduce the surface tension of the water, allowing it to adhere to the plate.

Oil-based inks

Because monotypes started in the etching studio, etching inks were the first inks used. Oil-based inks consist of finely ground pigment mixed with linseed oil. The particle size of the pigment is so small in this type of ink that very little oil is needed to make it spreadable. Linseed oil, because of its organic nature, can cause the cellulose of the printmaking paper to decompose as it ages. The less ink you use, therefore, the longer your prints will last. Lithograph inks are of similar composition and often have a small amount of varnish added to them to speed their drying. Both are good for monotypes and can create rich, dark colors and thin, translucent washes. Because of their density, oil-based inks often require the pressure from a printmaking press to give a good, dark impression.

Many artists today use regular oil paints to create monotypes. These paints are intended to be used with a brush. They have less finely ground particles and require more linseed oil to make them spreadable. Oil paints also contain fillers and other additives to give them specific characteristics. These and the extra oil can cause a rapid deterioration of the paper. As the print ages, a halo or butter-like stain will appear around certain colors as the linseed oil is absorbed into the paper. These extra ingredients also cause oil paints to spread more easily on the printmaking plate during printing. This can often lead to distortions of the image in the print.

SOLVENTS

Turpentine, kerosene and paint thinner are oil-based solvents. Kerosene is oily and is good for cleaning rubber rollers. It leaves a residual film of oil on the rubber which protects it from drying out. If you use kerosene to thin ink, the ink will create smooth, flowing washes and will dry slowly. Turpentine is a fast-drying solvent, good for thinning colors and for general cleanup, but odorless paint thinners are less toxic than turpentine and serve the same purposes. **SAFETY NOTE: Good ventilation is essential when using any solvent. Vapors from solvents are rapidly absorbed into the body and the liquid should never be allowed to come into contact with the skin. Gloves should be worn at all times when working with solvents.**

Janis Provisor, **Trophy**, *1989. Monotype with gold, copper and aluminum leaf; four panels, each 25 ¼ x 19 ½"*
(64 x 50 cm), total width 78" (198 cm). Courtesy Shark's Inc. (See page C 9 of the Color Gallery)

Janis Provisor, **About Face**, *1989. Color lithograph, woodcut, monotype with gold, copper and aluminum leaf; three panels,*
each 25 ¼ x 19 ½" (64 x 50 cm), total width 58 ½"(149 cm). Courtesy Shark's Inc. (See page C 9 of the Color Gallery)

Jan Arabas, **When Mahakala Comes**, *1986/87. Monotype, 12 sheets, each 30 x 40" (76 x 102 cm), total size 90 x 160"
(2.3 x 4.1 m). Courtesy the artist.*

PAPERS

There are many papers available for printing monotypes, from inexpensive newsprint to exotic tissues. Because the success of a print depends as much on the paper you choose as the image you make, you should experiment until you find the perfect match. Your experiments will help you determine the type of paper best suited to your images. For those with limited budgets, newsprint, construction paper,

bond paper and rolled wrapping paper can get you started with the process. If you find you can or want to try more expensive printing surfaces, move on to oatmeal, mulberry or rice papers.

Dampened paper should be strong enough to withstand handling and printing without tearing during the process. There are many thin Oriental tissues that would be too weak by themselves but could be laminated to a stronger sheet to create beautiful prints. This process, called *chine collé*,

is often used to tone areas of a print or to create strong color areas. Thin papers alone work best when printed dry, without a press. Stiff inks or heavy ink buildup may cause thin paper to rip as you are pulling the print away from the plate. Thicker, European-style papers work well with oil-based ink and when printed on a press. The wide variety of machine and handmade papers available today allow you to choose colors and textures to enhance your image.

THE PRINTING PROCESS: PREPARING PAPER AND PULLING A PRINT

1

At the beginning of the printing session, dampen your paper by running it through a tank of clean water. The wet sheets should be stacked on top of each other for forty-five minutes before printing.

2

*A dark field monotype can be made by removing ink from the plate. This can be done with tools, solvents, or even your fingers. **SAFETY NOTE: But be sure to wear gloves if you are using oil-based ink or paint.***

3

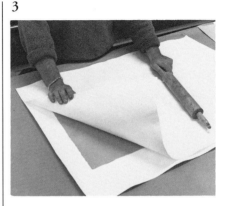

Before printing, the dampened paper must be rolled between blotters. This removes excess moisture that could cause distortion to your image by repelling ink.

4

The paper is laid on the inked plate…

5

…covered with felts and pressed. Monotypes can be pressed several times if necessary to darken the image.

6

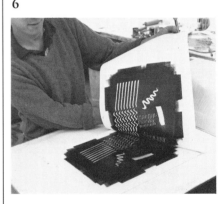

The paper is lifted from one edge to reveal the print.

REWORKING THE IMAGE

1

There is still enough ink on the plate for you to change the image and reprint it. Here, cut papers are being used as stencils to mask out inked areas.

2

The second print expands on the ideas in the first.

3

More changes can be made on the plate. The inked side of the paper stencils will also print if you turn them over and reprint the image.

4

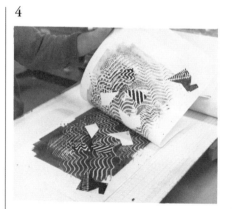

Each generation of the print becomes lighter unless fresh ink is applied.

5

The generational aspect of monotypes enhances tonal possibilities while providing many unexpected variations.

This print is the first impression of a reduction monotype. Joel Janowitz, **Still Life Series A/C**, *1989. Monotype, 29 ½ x 40 ½" (75 x 103 cm). Courtesy Rugg Road Paper & Prints. (See page C 10 of the Color Gallery)*

In this third generation print, color has been added to enhance areas that were softened by the previous printings. Joel Janowitz, **Still Life Series C/C**, *1989. Monotype with charcoal, 29 ½ x 40 ½" (75 x 103 cm). Courtesy Rugg Road Paper & Prints. (See page C 10 of the Color Gallery)*

*Maggi Brown, **Sans Letters**, 1990.*
Monotype, 29½ x 41½" (75 x 105 cm).
Courtesy Rugg Road Paper & Prints.

This second generation monotype has
been drawn on with oil pastel and pencil.
*Maggi Brown, **Two Forms**, 1990.*
Monotype, 29½ x 49½" (75 x 126 cm).
Courtesy Rugg Road Paper & Prints.

MULTIPLE-PRINT MONOTYPES

1

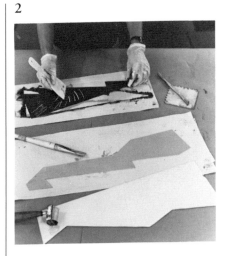

Artist Lois Beatty makes cardboard stencils for her multiple printed monotypes.

2

Each stencil is separately inked and textured.

3

Then they are fitted together on the plate and printed.

4

New stencils are inked and printed on top of the first layer until the final image is created. This often requires the print to be pressed six or seven times.

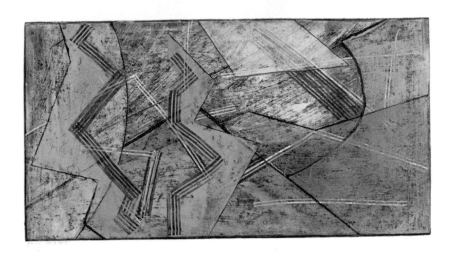

*Lois Beatty, **Turning Point XXIV**, 1989. Monotype, 10 x 19" (25 x 48 cm). Courtesy Rugg Road Paper & Prints.*

*This is another example of a multiple printed monotype. Yvonne Jacquette, **Speeding Tilted Night**, 1989. Color monotype, 30 x 22" (76 x 56 cm). Courtesy Shark's Inc. (See page C11 of the Color Gallery)*

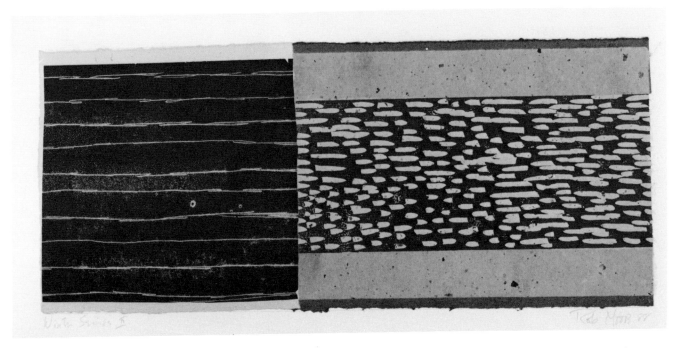

*Robert Moore, **Fall Series II -01**, 1988. Monotype using chine collé process, 9 x 21" (23 x 53 cm). Courtesy Rugg Road Paper & Prints.*

CHINE COLLÉ

The process of chine collé is an interesting way to experiment with a variety of papers. A number of glues can be used to attach lightweight papers to the print. Traditionally, wheat paste was used, but now methyl cellulose, wallpaper paste, PVA (polyvinyl acetate) or Elmer's library paste can be brushed onto the back of the lightweight paper. This paper is then placed on the inked printmaking plate, glue side facing up. The dampened printmaking paper (the base sheet) is laid across the papers on the printmaking plate. Additional sheets of newsprint are laid on the printmaking paper. These will absorb any excess ink or glue that might be forced through the paper during printing. This "sandwich" of papers is then run through the press. After pressing, the lightweight paper will remain glued to the base sheet if it is put between dry blotters and weighted. Waxed paper placed over the glued areas will prevent them from sticking to the blotters.

1

Papers that are too delicate to be used as printing surfaces by themselves can be printed and glued to regular weight printmaking paper in the chine collé process. Papers are placed glued side up on an inked plate.

2

Dampened printmaking paper is laid across the lightweight papers and the inked plate.

3

Newsprint sheets placed over the printmaking paper will absorb excess ink or glue forced through the paper during printing.

4

After pressing, the lightweight papers adhere to the printmaking paper, creating interesting textures and shapes.

1

Lisa Houck prepares a plate for a chine collé monoprint using etching plates. On etching plates, ink collects in the recessed areas of the plate. Ink is spread over the entire plate with stiff cardboard and forced into the recessed areas.

2

A stiff cloth called a tarlatan is used to wipe off excess ink.

3

A final cleaning of the surface is done with newspaper.

4

Glue is carefully applied to one side of every handmade paper shape. Working on pages of a phonebook allows a fresh surface for every paper shape.

5

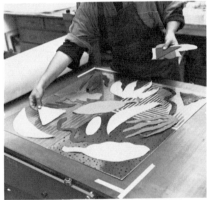

The shapes are laid on the inked etching plate, glue side up.

6

Damp paper is laid over the plate.

7

Pressing bonds the layers together and prints the surface.

8

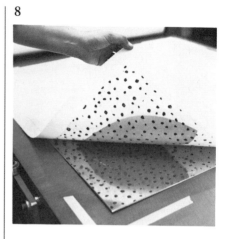

A multicolored and textured image is produced in one step.

9

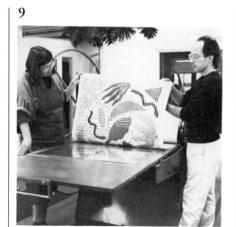

After the print is pulled from the plate, it is dried flat between blotters.

10

Lisa uses different shaped papers and different colored inks on each print. Each work is unique but based on a single fixed image on the plate. (See page C12 of the Color Gallery)

EXTENDING THE POSSIBILITIES

1

Melissa Johnson's prints are multiple printed, using found objects and unconventional drawing tools. Here she is "drawing" her image with masking tape on a broken Plexiglas plate.

2

The tape acts as a stencil and allows the colors from previously printed layers to show through. After she rolls ink over the plate, Johnson will remove the tape.

3

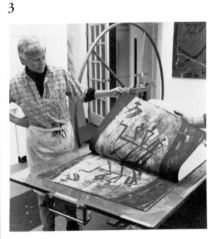

The paper is printed many times until the final image is achieved.

*Melissa Johnson, **Chalice #5**, 1990. Monotype, 43 x 30" (109 x 76 cm).*
Courtesy Rugg Road Papers & Prints.

CLAY MONOTYPES

1

Artist Mitch Lyons makes monotypes using clay as both printing plate and pigment. He prepares his plate by first stapling plastic sheeting onto a plywood frame. This makes it easier to remove the clay at a later time and keeps the clay from drying out.

2

He then presses porcelain clay into the plywood form.

3

The clay is flattened with a rolling pin.

4

Lyons creates his own colored clays, using 90% kaolin clay and 10% whiting (a common additive found in ceramic studios) as a binder.

5

Once the clay is in a liquid form containing the binder, the artist adds permanent pigments to the clay to create the printing colors.

6

He starts his pictures by brushing the colored clay onto newsprint and allowing it to dry.

7

The newsprint with its thin layer of clay is applied to the wet clay slab, which has been criss-crossed with masking tape stencils.

8

After layering on the colored clays, Lyons peels away the masking tape stencils, revealing a criss-crossed pattern.

9

More pigmented clay slip can be added with texturing tools like this carved roller.

10

Or brushed on with a stiff brush.

11

Dampened paper is laid gently on the finished image.

12

Pressure is applied with a rolling pin.

13

The image transfers to the paper.

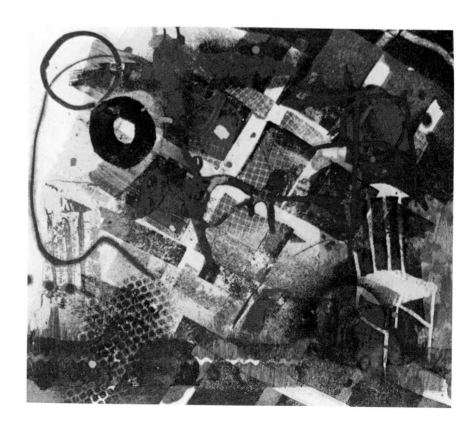

*The finished clay monotype. Mitch Lyons, **Untitled**, 1990. 14 x 18" (36 x 46 cm). Courtesy the artist.*

Pablo Picasso, **King of the Clowns**, *1965. Reduction linocut, 26 ⅛ x 20 ⅝" (67 x 52 cm) Courtesy Worcester Art Museum.*

linoleum 3

A good place to begin exploring relief print-making is on a piece of linoleum. This common, accessible material cuts easily and is inexpensive. Linoleum has a perfectly smooth surface without direction or grain. It can produce gracefully flowing lines and broad, flat areas of color. The surface is extremely receptive to indentations. Small textured objects such as tacks, pebbles or bits of wire can easily be pressed into it to create impressions that will print with the characteristic look of the object. Linoleum is also used in combination with other materials to make composite printing plates and to print flat areas of color behind more textured areas. The finished block is extremely durable and many hundreds of prints can be pulled without noticeable wear. Linoleum can also be etched with caustic soda

*Kyohei Inukai, **Mr. C**, no date. Linocut, 7½ x 6" (19 x 15 cm), edition of 250. Courtesy William Greenbaum Fine Prints.*

(sodium hydroxide) to produce either a relief or intaglio printing surface. This is not commonly done because the process takes several hours, but it can produce more variation in the linoleum's surface. Linoleum is so easy to manipulate that artists like Picasso and Matisse have used it for some of their most free-spirited prints.

TOOLS AND MATERIALS

Linoleum

You can buy linoleum for printmaking, premounted on plywood, in most art supply stores. The wood gives the linoleum more stability when you are cutting it, but the premounted pieces are generally quite small. Large sheets and rolls of battleship linoleum are available through most art materials catalogues, at floor covering showrooms

*T. L. Solein, **Untitled**, 1986. Linocut, 6 x 8" (15 x 20 cm), edition of 20. Courtesy the author.*

and some hardware stores or lumberyards. You can mount it easily on masonite or plywood with common white glue or acrylic medium, or you can use it unmounted. Cut large pieces to the required size with a sharp knife or a pair of heavy scissors. Scoring the linoleum with a knife and bending it over the edge of a table will cause it to break crisply. Shaped printmaking plates are also easy to make by cutting the linoleum with a knife. You can experiment with other types of floor tiles but most are too hard to cut with simple tools. **SAFETY NOTE: Use cutting tools with extreme care, and sharpen them regularly, as they rapidly become blunt when cutting linoleum.**

Over time, or in very cold weather, linoleum will harden and become difficult to carve. It can be made soft and pliable again by heating. This can be done by putting the linoleum block in a warm oven, lightly ironing it, or putting it in the sun for a few minutes until it becomes pliable. Use normal precautions for picking up hot objects, and don't leave it unattended.

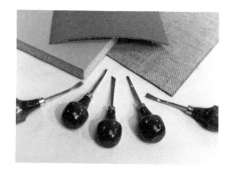

Linoleum is available in flat sheets or premounted on boards.

Linoleum can be scored with a sharp knife and folded over the edge of a table to break it into smaller pieces.

Linoleum can be easily cut to make shaped printmaking plates. Ted Dickerson pulls a shaped print on a Dickerson Press. This press has a unique interchangeable printing roll that allows you to print relief, intaglio and stone lithography on the same piece of equipment. Courtesy Dickerson Press Company, South Haven, Michigan.

*Linoleum has no grain. It is easy to cut in any direction and will give you smooth, curved lines. **Refer to safe cutting procedures on page 43.***

Cutting and sharpening

Traditional wood carving tools work well on linoleum. You can buy cutting tool sets for linoleum in art supply stores. Most come with a small handle and removable blades of many different sizes and shapes. Although linoleum is soft and easy to cut, it is also gritty in composition and will dull the cutting tools quickly. Dull tools take all of the fun out of this process. With sharp tools, you glide effortlessly in any direction through the linoleum. With dull tools, you'll want to go home early. Sharpening stones sharpen the backs and outside edges of the tools. Slipstones sharpen the inside edges. Have both stones on hand and use them often.

Ink

Both oil- and water-based inks can be used for printing linocuts. Light-fast pigments (those that do not fade with exposure to ultra-violet rays) are available in either form, and provide good coverage. Water-based inks dry faster, clean up more easily, and are safer for classroom situations. However, if your plate is large and you are using small brayers to ink it, remember that some areas may dry before you are ready to print. Oil-based inks, on the other hand, dry slowly both on the plate and on the finished print. Multiple printed images may take longer to produce because of this. **SAFETY NOTE: Because solvents are needed when working with oil-based inks, the work area must have adequate active ventilation. When not in use, oil-based inks must be stored in metal storage cabinets for safety. Gloves must be worn to prevent contact with the skin.**

Linoleum plates can become brittle with age. This aging can be slowed by cleaning the plate with kerosene rather than turpentine or odorless paint thinner. Kerosene leaves an oily film on the plate which will retard the aging process.

Paper

Different papers may be required for different stages of the printing process. To check the development of an image as you are carving it (known as "proofing the print"), newsprint is an inexpensive and sensible choice. It is a highly acidic paper, however, that will decompose over time and is not recommended for your final prints. The final choice of paper depends on your printing process and your ideas

*Steven Sorman, **Those From Away VII**, 1989. Linocut, 46¾ x 31¼" (119 x 79 cm), edition of 30. Printed and published by Tyler Graphics Ltd. Copyright Steven Sorman/Tyler Graphics Ltd., 1989. Photo: Steven Sloman.*

about the image you are printing. Smooth surfaced papers work well if large, flat areas of color are to be printed. Lightweight Oriental style papers work best if you are hand rubbing the print with a spoon or baren. Masa, gampi torinoko and kitakata are the names of a few of the many papers available. Heavier European style papers work well if you are printing on an etching press. Although most printmaking papers are white, you may want to explore the many toned and colored papers that are on the market. Your choice of paper is as important as your image. Linoleum prints can also be printed on cloth by either hand rubbing or press printing. The texture of the cloth greatly affects the image.

*Jane Kent, **Untitled**, 1989. Linoleum cut on buckram, 27 1/8 x 18 1/16"*
(69 x 46 cm). Courtesy Dolan/Maxwell New York. Photo: D. James Dee.

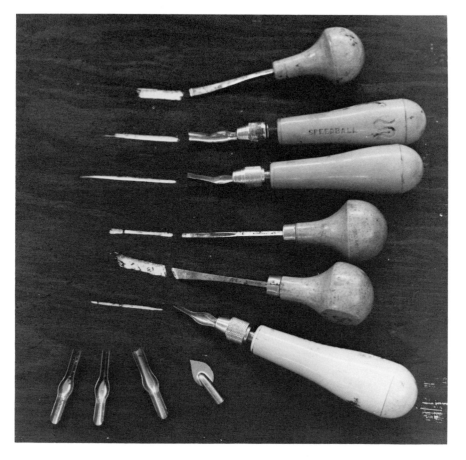

Basic linoleum carving tools are available in most art supply stores.

BASIC RELIEF PRINTMAKING PRACTICES

If linoleum cutting is new to you, it is a good idea to plan your image before you pick up a cutting tool. Experiment with black ink on white paper to get used to the strong contrasts possible with linoleum cuts. Work with large, simple shapes at first; add detail after you are accustomed to the cutting process and its results.

When you're ready to carve an image, you can either draw or paint it directly on the linoleum with ink or marker, or create a pencil drawing and transfer it to the block with carbon paper. Remember that any print is a mirror image of what you see on the block or plate. Keep in mind, too, that white areas are areas that will be cut away on the block.

SAFETY NOTE: Always cut away from your body. Keep the hand that does not hold the cutting tool out of the way of its sharp point. If possible, use a bench hook to brace the block and hold it in place as you cut (see page 74).

An economical and hassle-free way to proof your print is to make a crayon or soft pencil rubbing of the surface of the block. This will reveal areas that need additional work before you ink the block.

REDUCTION PRINTS

For most multicolored prints, a separate printing block is required for each color. Using a process called the reduction process you can produce multicolored prints by using only one piece of linoleum. This presents an interesting challenge for the artist.

The process is quite simple in concept. The print is developed from the lightest values to the darkest values. The first cuts made on the linoleum represent the lightest values in the image. Those areas are cut away and the plate is inked and printed. This layer usually has the least amount of cutting done in it. Each new layer of the image will be cut from what remains of the previous layer. New cuts are made in each layer to represent the next change in value. These are inked and printed over the previous layer. Consecutive cutting and printing establishes the darkest values of the image. Transparent inks can be used to create blended colors.

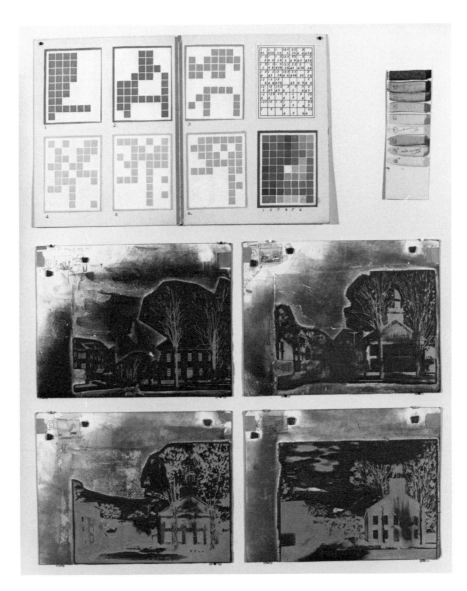

Eight separate blocks were required to make the print shown at the upper right. The grid chart refers to specific color relationships and the order of the printing. Samples of inks were also recorded for future color matching. (See page C12 of the Color Gallery)

The dark squares of cut linoleum on these blocks are registration points. Paper is placed next to these small pieces and the print is then hand rubbed.

Opaque inks mask out the ones beneath them. The final block represents the finest detail.

Because each new layer destroys the previous layer, there is no correcting of the image as it moves along. This can lead to unexpected changes in your plans as you progress through the printing process. If the process is approached methodically, great detail can be achieved. If a more freewheeling approach is taken, the unexpected may be extremely satisfying.

Another approach to this process is to separate an image photographically into many different values. There are photographic processes that can be used to layer these value changes onto linoleum or wood for reduction carving. Some require the use of a darkroom; others can be done with little or no equipment in normal lighting. There are many good manuals that deal with these processes and most of the products used come with fine instructions.

*Irving Amen, **Italian Landscape #3**, 1953. Reduction linocut, 12 x 15 ½" (30 x 39 cm). Courtesy William Greenbaum Fine Prints.*

Dennis Revitzky, **View of Laguna, New Mexico***, 1988 (detail). Linocut. Courtesy the artist.*

Michael Robbins, **Ancien de Mexico***, 1989. Color linoleum cut, 31 x 42" (79 x 107 cm), edition of 50. Courtesy Solo Edition. Photo: John Back.*

STATE AND PROGRESS PROOFS

These two proofing processes produce two distinctly different types of prints. State proofs show you what each layer of an image looks like by itself. Progress proofs show what each stage of the print looks like. Progress proof number four of a seven color print, for example, will show what the first four layers of color look like together. Number five shows five layers, and so on. This is clearly shown in the photo series of state and progress proofs of the linoleum print *Lucas*, by artist Chuck Close.

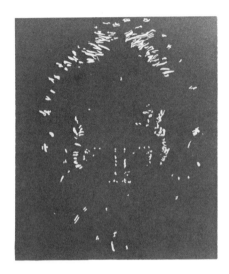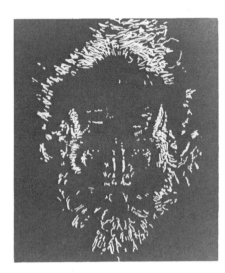

*These are the "state proofs" of the seven-step reduction print **Lucas, 1988** by Chuck Close. They show the amount of linoleum removed during each step of the print.*

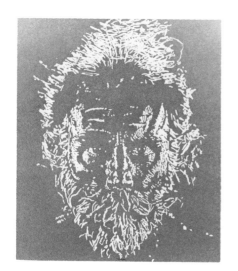
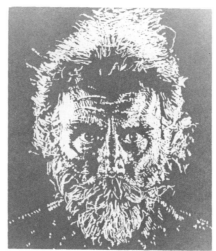
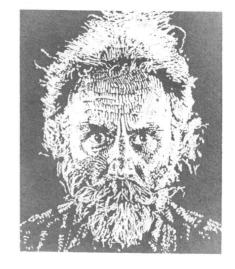

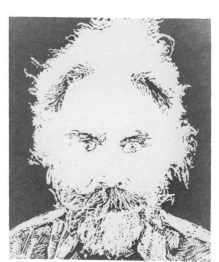

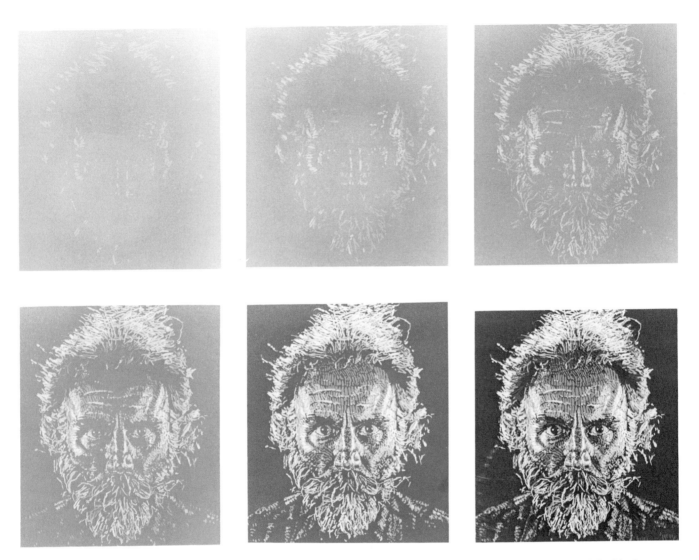

*These are the "progress proofs" of Close's reduction print, **Lucas, 1988**. They show the accumulated layering of the block as each color is printed. Image number five has the previous four layers beneath it, and so on. The final print is the accumulation of all seven layers.*

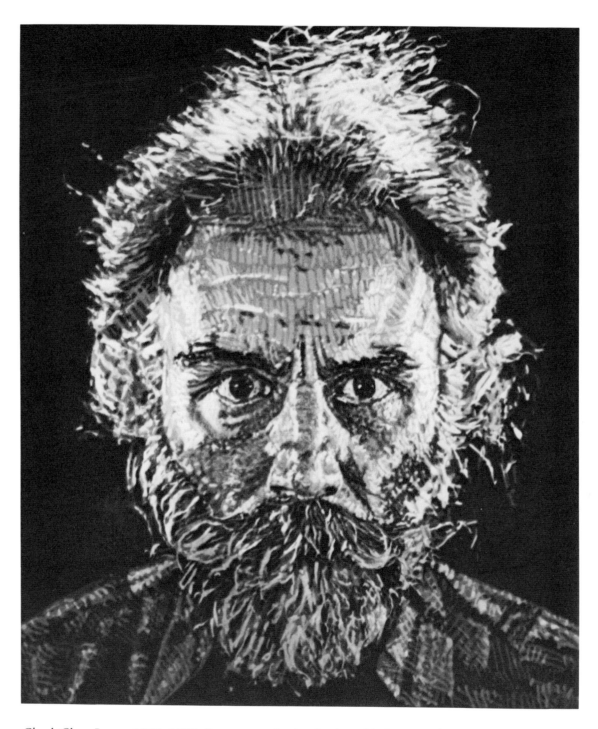

*Chuck Close, **Lucas, 1988**, 1989. Seven-step reduction linoleum block print, 14 ½ x 12 ½" (37 x 32 cm). Courtesy Pace Editions. Photo: John Back.*

Chuck Close, **Janet, 1988,** *1989. Seven-step reduction linoleum block print, 14½ x 12½" (37 x 32 cm). Courtesy Pace Editions. Photo: John Back.*

*Michael Hurson, **A Dog and a Frog**, no date. Linoleum cut. Courtesy Grenfell Press. Photo: D. James Dee.*

*Rob Moore, **Fall Series #17**, 1987. Linocut with chine collé, 5 ½ x 20 ½" (14 x 52 cm). Courtesy Rugg Road Papers & Prints.*

*Randal Thurston, **Calvary**, 1990. Cardboard print, 76 x 114" (1.9 x 2.9 m). Courtesy Akin Gallery, Boston.*

cardboard 4

One of the joys of relief printmaking is the wide variety of materials with which prints can be made. Things that most people throw away can produce fascinating and unusual effects. Cardboard is a good example. Readily available in innumerable sizes, thicknesses and compositions, cardboard is also cheap and versatile, an obvious choice for artists or schools with limited budgets and fertile imaginations.

TOOLS AND MATERIALS

Ordinary cardboard can be used as a printing surface in a variety of ways. Like linoleum, cardboard is easy to texture with harder materials. Nails, wire, paper clips and pebbles can be forced against the surface to make impressions that will print. A simple tool such as a screwdriver or an etching needle can be pulled across its surface to make an indentation. These marks will print as white lines when the surface of the block is inked. Because of its fibrous qualities, cardboard is difficult to carve, but corrugated cardboard is made up of layers that present interesting possibilities. The outer layer of brown paper can be cut into and peeled back to reveal the striped inner structure. This can be inked and printed in contrast to the flat surface.

Shapes cut from cardboard can be fit together jigsaw puzzle style. They can be inked separately to make a multiple colored print. Thick cardboard can also be used to create embossing when printed on damp paper with a press. The surface of the cardboard can be coated with gesso or acrylic medium to give it texture. Other materials — cloth, wire screening, sandpaper, crumpled paper — can be glued to it. This plate can be printed relief or intaglio style.

1

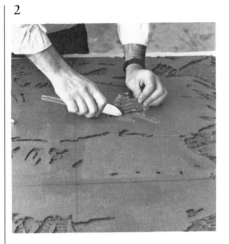

Randal Thurston draws first, then cuts shapes from the top layer of corrugated cardboard to create his printing plate.

2

The middle, rippled layer is removed when he wants to print clear areas. It is left and printed when he wants a textured look.

3

*Polyurethane seals the cardboard to make a harder and less absorbent surface. **SAFETY NOTE: Use polyurethane only in well-ventilated areas. Follow manufacturer's instructions carefully.***

4

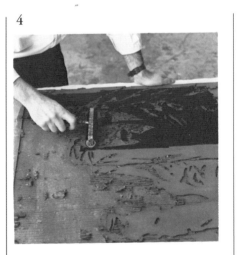

Ink is rolled on with a brayer.

5

The paper is hand rubbed with a wooden spoon.

6

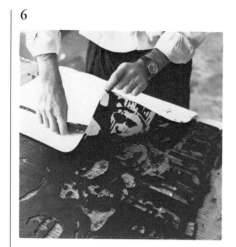

The image transfers easily.

7

Randal prints on many small sheets of paper and then assembles them to make the final composition. These elements can be glued but are often stapled or nailed to a board for the final presentation.

A printed image (left) and its cardboard plate.

PREPARING THE PLATE

Cardboard may distort if water comes in contact with it. For this reason, a cardboard plate lasts longest if printed with oil-based inks. Any cardboard plate, however, used with any ink must be sealed to prevent distortion during printing. Acrylic gel medium, gesso or polyurethane varnish seal it well when applied in a thin layer. Inked plates can be hand rubbed or printed on an etching press.

A variety of corrugated cardboard plates.

These carved, shaped and selectively inked cardboard plates were printed and then used as stencils for freehand shadowing around the images. Irving Amen, **Haystacks in the South of France**, *no date. Cardboard relief print, 28 x 16" (71 x 41 cm), edition of 15. Courtesy William Greenbaum Fine Prints.*

*Paul Gauguin, **Nave Nave Fenua**, no date. Woodcut, 14 x 8" (36 x 20 cm). Courtesy Museum of Fine Arts, Boston. Bequest of W. G. Russell Allen.*

woodblocks 5

A BIT OF BACKGROUND

Woodblock printing is one of the earliest and simplest of the print-making techniques. It is also one of the most enduring, having been in constant use for centuries.

You draw the image for a woodblock print on the plank or long grained side of a board. The areas of the image that will not be printed are removed by cutting away the wood. Ink is applied to the raised areas and the image is printed in reverse on paper or cloth either by hand rubbing or with a press.

Woodblock prints have recorded people's lives and beliefs since early times. With the invention of paper-making in 105 AD, religious images of all kinds were spread to believers. The earliest document on paper is thought to be a Chinese scroll known as the Dharma Sutra. This

*Louisa Chase, **Thicket**, 1982. Black and white woodcut, 30 x 36" (76 x 91 cm), edition of 10. Courtesy Diane Villani Editions, New York.*

seventeen-foot-long scroll of paper was printed with a multiple colored woodblock prayer — evidence that the Chinese had a long history of block printing. Lightweight Oriental papers were ideal for this hand rubbed printmaking process.

Block printing in Europe was first used for textile design. It wasn't until the 1400s that hand paper-making developed sufficiently as an industry to produce printed images for religious and secular purposes. Because the general population at that time was illiterate, pictures were used to spread information. Simple images were printed in black on white paper and then hand colored. These carried the messages of people and their gods. Block printing was also part of the leisure life of the times. Playing cards with printed pictures on them became popular in the early 1400s.

In the earliest books, both words and illustrations were cut into a single block for each page. With the invention of movable type, block printed illustrations could stand alone, and they moved quickly into

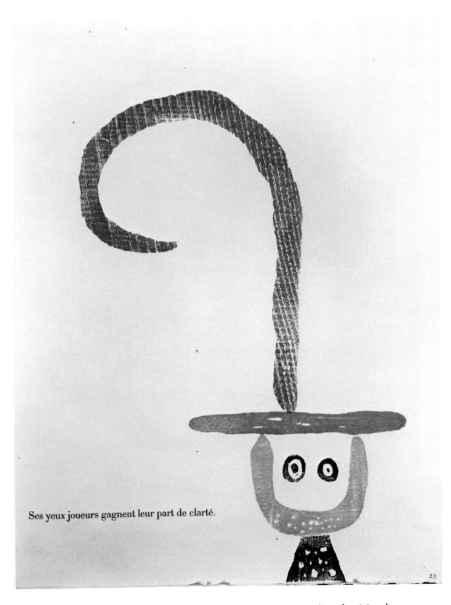

Ses yeux joueurs gagnent leur part de clarté.

*Joan Miró, One illustration from the book **A Toute Epreuve** (2 vols., 80 color woodcuts). Courtesy Museum of Fine Arts, Boston. Seth K. Sweetser Fund.*

the broader, secular world. In 1486, Dutch artist Erhard Reuwich created a five-foot-long print depicting the city of Venice. This jump in scale took printing into the realm of painting as a medium for creating large images. It also acknowledged the printmaker as an artist and not just as a technician. Today, centuries later, woodblock prints are still prized for their clean, straightforward look, and are widely used in book and magazine illustration.

The physical process of carving makes woodblock an excellent medium for vigorous expressionism. Graphic images in wood have often been used to express political upheaval and social strife, and have inspired social activists around the world. The political graphics of the Mexican Revolution of 1910-1920 are among the boldest examples of this style ever produced. By contrast, wood's seductive textures and grains also suit it for the most spiritual and transcendental of graphic images. Both descriptive Japanese woodcuts from the early 1800s and modern abstract woodcuts by artists such as Helen Frankenthaler owe much of their beauty to the soft textural surface of the wood on which they are carved.

*A.R. Penck, **Untitled #5** from "8 Erfahungen," 1981. Black and white woodcut, 31 ½ x 23 ½" (80 x 60 cm). Courtesy Peter Blum Editions.*

*A.R. Penck, **Untitled #3** from "8 Erfahungen," 1981. Black and white woodcut, 31 ½ x 23 ½" (80 x 60 cm). Courtesy Peter Blum Editions.*

*A.R. Penck, **Untitled #7** from "8 Erfahungen," 1981. Black and white woodcut, 31 ½ x 23 ½" (80 x 60 cm). Courtesy Peter Blum Editions.*

The perfect woodblock plate will often be something at hand. These loosely inked plates are made from table tops in the artist's studio. The drawing was done with an electric router. The plates were inked with wood stain and hand rubbed. Nigel Rolfe, (left to right) **Tools of the Trade, The Garden, The Worker,** *1989. Woodblock prints, unique proofs, 104 x 55 ½" (2.6 x 1.4 m). Courtesy Dolan/Maxwell, New York.*

CHOOSING WOOD

Your choice of wood depends on the type of image you are making. With care, you can transfer texture and image just as effectively from a tree trunk as from a beautiful piece of cherry board. Plywood is available with many different types of wood laminated to its surface. Weathered barn boards will create an effect dif-ficult to achieve any other way. A shaped bread board is already charged with information.

Soft woods

From a lumberyard, pine is the most commonly available wood and the softest. It splinters easily, so a sharp tool is required to cut across its grain. It is often filled with knots — a char-acteristic which can add to or detract from the beauty of your image. The surface of a piece of pine can be made harder (and consequently easier to cut) by coating it with a dilute mixture of polyurethane or shellac. Polyurethane can be thinned with turpentine or odorless thinner; shellac can be thinned with alcohol. A mixture of half solvent and half hardener is adequate for this purpose without changing the quality of the wood. **SAFETY NOTE: Use these products only outdoors or in areas with active ventilation. Follow manufacturer's instructions. If polyurethane or other solvents are used, gloves should be worn.**

The natural tendency when cutting a woodblock is to make straight rather than curved lines, following the grain of the board. Soft woods are difficult to cut fine lines into and these lines often become compressed or damaged during printing. On the other hand, soft wood is easy to texture and distress for more random marks. Sugar pine is the best of the available varieties.

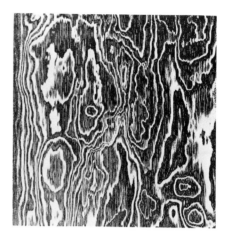

Wood can be sandblasted to enhance the look of its grain when printed.

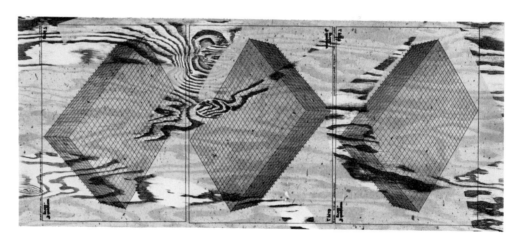

*This print shows the effect of an enhanced grain on an image. Steve Keister, **Reverse Angle Replay,** 1989. Woodcut, chine collé, silkscreen, 24 x 56" (61 x 142 cm), edition of 45. Courtesy Solo Impression.*

Medium-soft woods

Poplar and bass are medium-soft woods that are readily available and are often used in furniture construction and in artists' drawing boards. They have an even texture and are easily cut with or against the grain. They will take fine cutting and withstand multiple printings without wear.

Hard woods

Fruit woods are among the finest surfaces for carving. Cherry, pear and apple are available, although you may have to do some searching to find them. They are hard, fine-textured, even-grained and excellent for carving fine textures and lines. Cherry is the traditional choice of Japanese printers. Most of these woods come in narrow width boards. They can be glued side by side with others to create a print of any scale.

Oak, another hard wood, is too hard for easy cutting. It has an open grain that does not lend itself to fine line work or flat areas of color.

Laminated woods

Large scale prints can be achieved with the use of plywood, which commonly comes in four-foot by eight-foot sheets, but can be ordered in five-foot by ten-foot size as well. Pine and fir on plywood have strong grains which can be enhanced with a wire brush to create dramatic texture. Exotic woods are also available laminated onto plywood. Birch is a common surface available in most lumberyards and produces good detail and fine cutting. It also produces flat areas of color with minimal texture on large prints.

The hard, smooth, textureless surface of masonite can also be used as a large primary cutting surface. In a two-color print, it can also be used as an additional printing plate. It will produce flat areas of color behind a more textured image.

Warping

Woodblocks sometimes warp. This is less of a problem if you are hand rubbing the block to print it, or if you are using plywood, which warps less often because of its multilayered construction. It is a major problem, however, if you are printing on a press. The risk of the block warping is reduced by attaching a strip of wood to the end of the block perpendicular to the grain of the block. This can be done with tongue and groove joinery or by gluing and nailing the strip in place. If you are going to attach a strip to your block, do it before you start cutting the design.

PAPER

The method of printing is a major factor in determining the type of paper that you need for any relief print. If the plate is to be hand rubbed, thin Oriental papers work well. The pressure from simple tools like a spoon or baren will easily transfer the ink to the paper to produce clean images. If you are using an etching or letter press, you should use heavier papers. Machine-made, European style papers are available in sheets and rolls. The rolls allow you to cut the paper to the size you need. This will allow you to make prints of great dimension. Handmade papers are smaller, seldom larger than thirty inches by forty inches in either European or Oriental style. Several contemporary American hand papermills produce custom papers for artists (see *Suppliers,* page 139). These papers generally stay within the thirty-inch by forty-inch range.

Experimenting with many papers is a worthwhile part of printing your image. Paper plays a major role in all graphic images and should be considered carefully. Many nationally advertised paper suppliers provide mail order service (see Suppliers). It is well worth your effort to contact them.

A variety of papers can be used for printing woodblock prints.

*John Buck, **Crossroads**, 1987. Woodcut, 74 x 36" (188 x 91 cm), edition of 15. Courtesy Shark's Inc.*

*John Buck, **Capetown**, 1987. Woodcut, 74 x 37" (188 x 94 cm), edition of 15. Courtesy Shark's Inc.*

Michael Duffy, **Cane Factory***, 1986.
Woodcut, 48 x 32" (122 x 81 cm),
edition of 10. Courtesy Shark's Inc.*

*Michael Duffy, **Fields**, 1986.
Woodcut, 48 x 32" (122 x 81 cm),
edition of 10. Courtesy Shark's Inc.*

TOOLS FOR CUTTING AND SHARPENING

Anything harder than wood can be used to make a mark in a woodblock that will print white. Simple objects such as nails, leather decorating tools, pizza cutters or a screwdriver can be forced against the surface of the wood. An electric drill or a dremel tool can be used to draw with. When predictability and control are required, traditional wood carving equipment is helpful.

Knives

A sharp, carbon steel knife and a sharpening stone are indispensable in woodblock printmaking. The knife should be comfortable to hold. The edge should be sharp and straight and the tip pointed for cutting small detail. The knife will cut straight lines with or across the grain. It can be used for creating texture as well as shapes. The knife is held like a pencil for making detailed cuts. It is grasped firmly and carefully pulled toward you when making deep cuts. It is best to make several passes with the knife when making a mark rather than one deep cut. The energy required for deep cutting will tire you of the

A variety of inexpensive woodcutting tools.

process in a short time. Keep your tools sharp and let them do the work. **SAFETY NOTE: Don't exhaust yourself too early in the process. Keep in mind that a sharp tool will cut you more easily — be careful. Always try to cut away from your body.**

To make a line that will print with clean distinction, you will need to cut a V-shaped sliver out of the wood. Most often this is done by cutting the block in one direction and then turning the block around and cutting from the other direction.

Chisels and gouges should always be directed away from the body.

Left to right: Veiners, used to create line and textural detail; gouges, used for clearing broad areas; knives, used for defining shapes.

Gouges can be used to clear areas between shapes and to make expressionistic marks.

With a little patience, you can train your hand to make both cuts from the same side. Although awkward at first, it will save you time once you've mastered the technique. Avoid undercuts, which will collapse when printed and fill with ink during the cleaning of the block. Knives can be used to texture, scrape and score the wood surface. Whole compositions can be created with no other tool. The knife can be used to delineate the edge of a large area that is to be removed. The wood can then be removed with a chisel or gouge.

Chisels

A chisel is used for removing rough, uneven texture from areas that will print white and to clear large areas of wood. Chisels are used across the grain when clearing large areas. They are sometimes unpredictable when used with the grain — they may remove too much wood by splintering. Regular carpenter's chisels in widths from ⅛" to ½" are useful for many purposes. Like knives, they must be kept sharp at all times for effortless cutting.

V Tools

V tools, called veiners, are cutters used for creating line. They serve the same function as a knife in creating a space in the wood that will print as a white area. Cuts with the V tool and the chisel are made by cutting away from the body. An assortment of these tools in different sizes is helpful. Larger versions are made for wood sculpture and furniture making, and are intended to be used with a mallet. Depending on the scale of your print, you may want the larger versions as well as the smaller ones.

Gouges

Tools with curved blades are called gouges and come in different widths. They are designed for making deep or wide cuts, usually to clear areas between the shapes in the image or to create texture. They are designated as C or U gouges depending on the shape of the curve of the blade. U gouges are used for making deep cuts and must be kept absolutely sharp to be efficient. Cuts are made away from the body and in the direction of the grain. You should use several sizes to prevent the image from becoming marked monotonously with cuts of a consistent size.

Sharpening stones

Sharpening stones are of two kinds. Preliminary sharpening is done on a carborundum stone. Final sharpening is done on an Arkansas or India stone. Only sharpen the edge of the tool that has already been sharpened. You will know this by its highly polished edge. Each tool has a specific side that is sharp and gives the tool its special quality. Patience and care must be taken to learn to sharpen V, U and C gouges. Follow the instructions included with your sharpening stone. It is essential that cutting tools be sharp and it takes a little practice to get them that way.

OTHER ESSENTIAL EQUIPMENT

It is important that the wood you are working with is held firmly in place while you carve. This is for your own safety as well as the accuracy of the marks you are making. For small work, a bench hook is a simple and easy solution to this problem. It is made from plywood to which strips of one-inch-thick wood have been attached to the top and bottom sides on opposite faces. One strip of wood holds the bench hook from sliding on the table. The other keeps the wood block from sliding on the bench hook. An improvement on this simple bench hook involves a grid of drilled holes and a right-angled cut piece of plywood. Dowels drilled and glued into the right-angled wooden piece can be fitted into the holes to make a movable corner. This allows the carver to adjust the angle of the board for more comfortable cutting. If you can drill holes directly into your table top, this adjustable corner can be fit into these.

If you are working on a large piece of plywood, carpenter's C clamps will hold the board to your table. You will need to protect the board from becoming indented by these clamps. This can be done by placing a piece of heavy cardboard or another thin piece of wood on the printing surface before the clamps are attached.

A heavy work bench or heavy table is important when you are

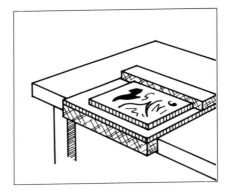

A simple bench hook can be easily assembled.

*The unique character of the line in this image was created using an electric drill as the carving tool. Irving Amen, **Unique Print**, 1953. Woodblock print, 24 x 9 ½" (61 x 24 cm). Courtesy William Greenbaum Fine Prints.*

carving. The activity of carving and pounding can cause a lightweight table to move across the floor. Placing the table next to a wall will stop this movement. Lightweight tables also make noise when a mallet is used with a chisel or gouge. If possible, nail woodblocks directly onto the table or bench during the carving process.

TEXTURING THE BLOCK

Many things can be used to create marks in the wood that will print. The search for such objects and tools is often an enjoyable part of planning the design for the print. Hard objects like nails, washers, pebbles, paper clips and bottle caps can be forced into the wood either by hand or with the help of the etching press. When using the press, however, you must be careful to protect the roller from becoming damaged. This can be done by placing a thin sheet of plywood or sheet metal over the woodblock and the objects. This sandwich of materials can be run through the press at a light pressure to mark the wood surface.

*This print is an encyclopedia of textures available to the woodblock printmaker. Irving Amen, **Geometry**, 1940. Woodblock print, 21 x 16" (53 x 41 cm). Courtesy William Greenbaum Fine Arts.*

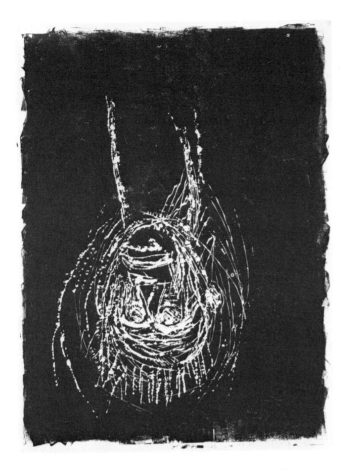

*George Baslitz, **Head**, 1982. Woodblock, 79 x 59"
(2 x 1.5 m). Courtesy The Alpha Gallery, Boston.*

*Emil Nolde, **Prophet**, 1912. Woodcut, 12 ½ x 9"
(32 x 23 cm). Courtesy The Alpha Gallery, Boston.*

Electric drills can be used with a variety of adjustable attachments. Steel wire brush attachments rapidly remove the wood's soft tissue and create strong grain effects. Steel wool and wire brushes can also be used to enhance the look of the grain. Drill bits can be used as drawing tools to create unexpected lines and textures. A sanding disk attachment for an electric drill can quickly change the texture on an area of a weathered board.

An electric jigsaw is an important tool in the relief print studio. It is used to change the shape of the board and can make complicated shapes for multiple color printing. A small electric router can also be useful for making lines.

SAFETY NOTE: You must be sure to secure the wood to the table before using any power tool on it. The action of the power tool can easily throw the board across the room unless it is held firmly in place with a C clamp or other device. Be sure to wear protective goggles at all times when working with power tools.

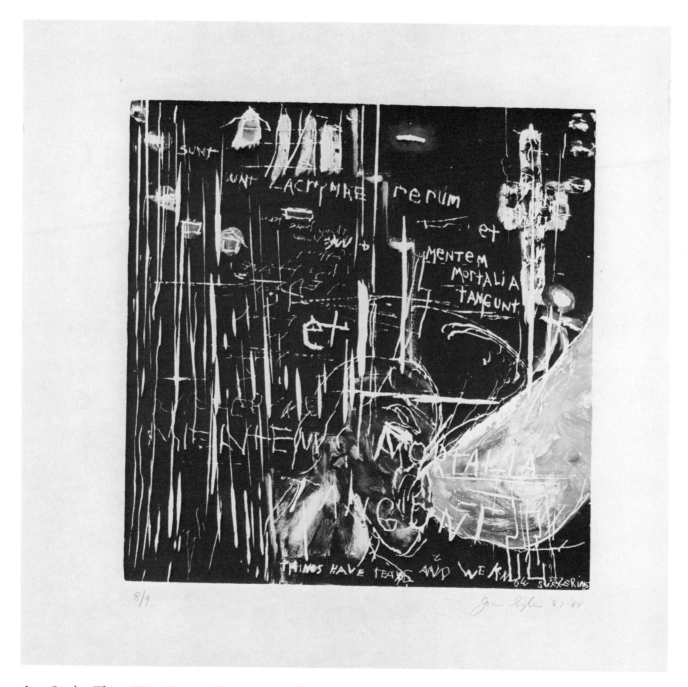

*Joan Snyder, **Things Have Tears and We Know Suffering**, 1984. Woodcut, 26 x 25" (66 x 64 cm), edition of 9. Courtesy Diane Villani Editions, New York. Photo: Steven Sloman.*

Cutting on the hard end grain gives great detail to small images.

Woodblock engravings were often used for commercial illustrations and typography.

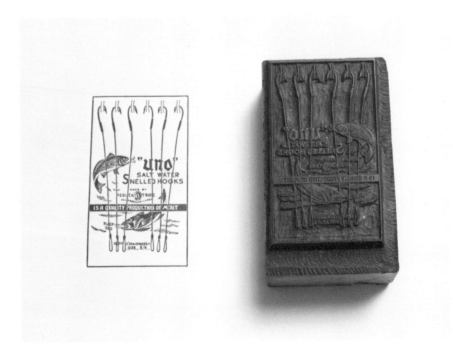

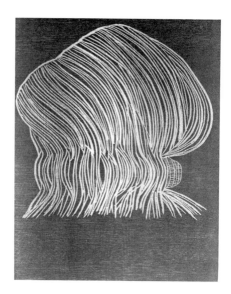
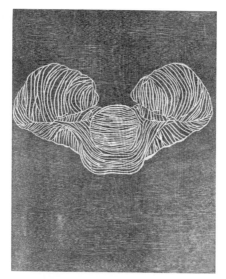
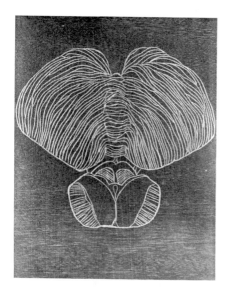

Terry Winters, **Furrows**, *1989, a suite of five woodcuts. Woodblock prints, 27 x 21 ¼ " (69 x 54 cm), edition of 45. Courtesy Peter Blum Editions. Photo: Zindman/Fremont.*

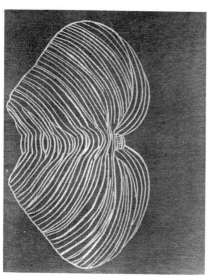

*John Torreano, **Emerald** from "Oxygems," suite of five prints, 1989. Color woodblock with embossing, 30 x 36" (76 x 91 cm). Courtesy Solo Impression.*

*The enhanced grain of the woodblock plate imparts a distinct texture to the print. John Torreano, **Emerald** (detail), 1989. Courtesy Solo Impression.*

Louisa Chase, **Black Sea**, 1983.
Black and white woodcut, 30 x 36"
(76 x 91 cm), edition of 10. Courtesy
Diane Villani Editions, New York.

Francesco Clemente, **Febbre Alta**,
1982. Woodcut, 26 ¾ x 21 ¼"
(68 x 54 cm), edition of 35.
Courtesy Peter Blum Editions.

Francesco Clemente, **Febbre Alta**,
1982. Woodcut, 26 ¾ x 21 ¼"
(68 x 54 cm), edition of 35.
Courtesy Peter Blum Editions.

James Brown, **Untitled Woodcut,** *1986. Woodcut, 18 x 17" (46 x 43 cm), edition of 27.*
Courtesy Pace Editions.

*Jim Dine, **The Mead of Poetry #1**, 1988. Woodcut/chine collé, 48 x 34"
(122 x 86 cm), edition of 15. Courtesy Pace Editions.*

PLACING THE IMAGE ON THE BLOCK

Direct application

The process of putting the image on the block to be cut will vary according to your personal style. You can draw or paint directly onto the wood. Although preliminary drawing can be done with a pencil, water-based paints or inks used with a brush, or felt-tipped markers give a similar look to that of the final print. They also dry quickly so you can start to carve right away. Corrections can be made by rubbing with a damp sponge or with light sandpaper. Drawing with charcoal also reveals the texture of the grain of the wood and gives a look similar to the print. The drawn lines show the areas that will remain after the wood is carved away. These are usually the positive shapes in the image.

Another approach is to cover the surface of the board with a dark color. This can be India ink or printing ink rubbed on with a cloth. This thin, dark layer will reveal some of the grain and imperfections in the wood. The drawing, done with light-colored paint or crayon, can be used to show the negative areas in the print. With either

Prints involving several techniques can be done in sections. Here, Ken Tyler and Frank Stella cut out metal pieces that will be collaged onto plywood to be used for a plate in the Swan Engraving series at Tyler Graphics Ltd. Photo courtesy Tyler Graphics Ltd.

The pieces are inked separately and assembled for printing. Photo courtesy Tyler Graphics Ltd.

*Frank Stella, **Swan Engraving Square II**, 1982. Relief, etching, 53 ½ x 52" (136 x 132 cm), edition of 20. Printed and published by Tyler Graphics Ltd. Copyright Frank Stella/Tyler Graphics Ltd., 1982. Photo: Steven Sloman.*

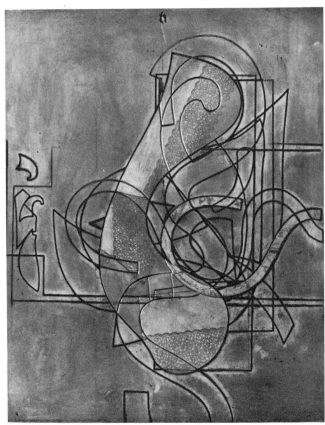

*These two plates are combination wood and metal printmaking plates. The metal plate is etched and inked intaglio style. The wood is carved and inked relief style. They are blocks for Frank Stella's print **Pergusa Three**. Courtesy Tyler Graphics Ltd. Photo copyright Kenneth E. Tyler.*

*Irene Valencius, **Untitled #59**, 1989. Monotype, 22 x 29" (56 x 74 cm).
Courtesy the artist and Rugg Road Papers & Prints.*

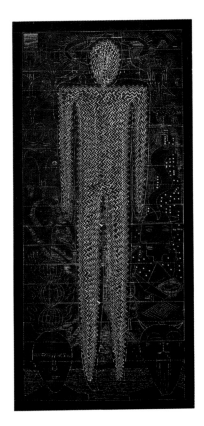

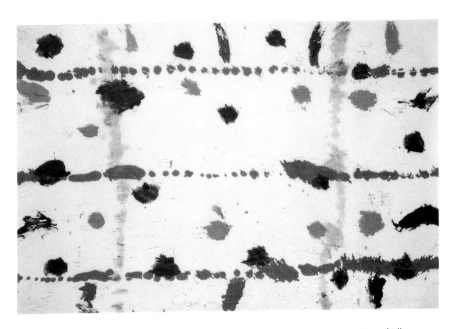

Stanley Boxer, **Pathofspentpassion**, 1989. Woodcut monoprint, 32 x 48"
(81 x 122 cm). Courtesy Smith Andersen Editions.

John Buck, **Red Jesus**, 1986. Color
woodcut, 72½ x 36½"(184 x 93 cm),
edition of 30. Courtesy Shark's Inc.

Ida Applebroog, **Promise I Won't Die?**, 1987. Hand-colored lithograph and
linoleum cut, 36 x 48" (91 x 122 cm), edition of 45. Courtesy Solo Impression.

Peter Halley, *A Tour of the Monuments of Passaic, New Jersey*, 1989.
*Magnesium line etching printed relief style, 16 x 20" (41 x 51 cm). Courtesy
The Spring Street Workshop.*

James Surls, *Cut Hand, Hurt Eyes*,
*1990. Woodcut, 72 x 36" (183 x 91 cm).
Courtesy Houston Fine Art Press.*

Betty Woodman, *Shadow*, 1987. Color monotype collage, 32 x 48" (81 x 122 cm).
Published by Shark's Inc., Boulder, CO. Courtesy Shark's Inc.

Michael David, **Invisible Cities**,
*1988. Woodcut, collagraph,
27 ¼ x 20 ½" (69 x 52 cm), edition
of 23. Courtesy Pace Editions.*

Louisa Chase, **Red Sea**, *1983. Color woodcut, 33 x 38 ½" (84 x 98 cm), edition
of 25. Courtesy Diane Villani Editions.*

Tony King, **Twenty Dollar Bill**, *1981. Silkscreen, 15 x 35" (38 x 89 cm). Courtesy Preston Graphics.*

Paul Laffoley, **Geochronmechane**, 1990. Silkscreen, 28 x 28" (71 x 71 cm).
Courtesy Preston Graphics.

Derek Boshier, **Guardians**, 1987.
Linocut, 64 x 40 ½" (163 x 103 cm).
Courtesy Houston Fine Art Press.

Eric Avery, **Les Demoiselles
d'Avignon de San Ygnacio**, 1984.
Woodblock print on offset poster, 28 x 26"
(71 x 66 cm). Courtesy the artist.

*Todd McKie, **Party Trick**, 1989. Monotype, 22 x 27"
(56 x 69 cm). Courtesy the artist and Rugg Road Papers
& Prints.*

*Jane Kent, **Untitled**, 1989. Linocut on buckram, 66 x 48"
(168 x 122 cm). Courtesy Dolan/Maxwell, New York.*

*Jane Kent, **Untitled**, 1989. Unique
print, linocut on fabric, 40 x 30"
(102 x 76 cm). Courtesy
Dolan/Maxwell, New York.*

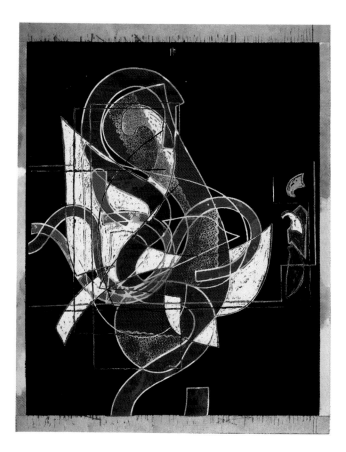

Frank Stella, **Pergusa Three**, 1983. Relief, woodcut and handmade, hand-colored paper, 66 x 52" (168 x 132 cm), edition of 30. Printed and published by Tyler Graphics Ltd. Copyright Frank Stella/Tyler Graphics Ltd., 1983.

Steven Sorman, **Those From Away IV**, 1989. Woodcut, 20 ½ x 18 ¼" (52 x 46 cm), edition of 26. Printed and published by Tyler Graphics Ltd. Copyright Steven Sorman/Tyler Graphics Ltd., 1989.

*Christine Kidder, **Endangered Hawksbill Turtle**. Silkscreen, 25 x 25" (64 x 64 cm). Courtesy Preston Graphics.*

*Richard Bosman, **Rapids**, 1987. Color woodcut, 42 x 37½" (107 x 95 cm), edition of 35. Courtesy Diane Villani Editions.*

*Charles Hewitt, **Iago II**, 1989. Woodcut, 46 x 34" (117 x 86 cm), edition of 9. Courtesy Vinalhaven Press.*

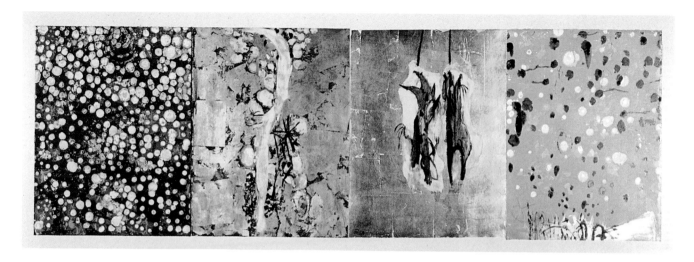

*Janis Provisor, **Trophy**, 1989. Monotype with gold, copper and aluminum leaf; four panels, each 25 ¼ x 19 ½" (64 x 50 cm), total width 78" (198 cm). Courtesy Shark's Inc. (See also page 18.)*

*Janis Provisor, **About Face**, 1989. Color lithograph, woodcut, monotype with gold, copper and aluminum leaf; three panels each 25 ¼ x 19 ½" (64 x 50 cm), total width 58 ½" (149 cm). Courtesy Shark's Inc. (See also page 18.)*

*Joel Janowitz, **Still Life Series A/C**, 1989. Monotype 29 ½ x 40 ½" (75 x 103 cm). Courtesy Rugg Road Paper & Prints. (See also page 22.)*

*Joel Janowitz, **Still Life Series C/C**, 1989. Monotype 29 ½ x 40 ½" (75 x 103 cm). Courtesy Rugg Road Paper & Prints. (See also page 22.)*

Yvonne Jacquette, **Speeding Tilted Night,** *1989. Color monotype, 30 x 22" (76 x 56 cm). Courtesy Shark's Inc.*
(See also page 25.)

*Lisa Houck, **Traveling North to See an Eclipse,** 1989. Chine collé monoprint, 36 x 36" (91 x 91 cm). Courtesy of the author. (See also page 29.)*

Grid charts like this one are used to plan the printing of a reduction print (see page 44).

approach, the direct application of the drawing onto the board usually gives loose guidelines for the carver and more spontaneity to the process. Images drawn on the board will appear in reverse on the print, a basic premise of print design. The disadvantage of direct drawing is that you never get to see what the image really looks like until you print it. This can be partially overcome by holding the board up to a mirror. The image you see in the mirror will closely approximate the printed image.

Transfer methods

If your image is complex and requires the precise copying of detail, transferring a drawing onto the block is your best approach. Simple methods of tracing and off-setting will produce good results. Photocopy machines can produce exact reproductions. Because the transfer method reverses the image on your block, the print will appear the same as your drawing. Here are a few examples.

To transfer a photocopied image, lacquer thinner is brushed onto a small area of the board. The photocopy is rubbed from the back and the image transfers. Lacquer thinner dries quickly so only small areas should be done at a time. Taping the drawing in place will assure exact registration of the process. **SAFETY NOTE: Use lacquer thinner only in areas with active ventilation. Follow all manufacturer's precautions. In classroom situations it is recommended that respirators and gloves be worn.**

Charcoal offset: If the design can be created in charcoal or colored chalk, this approach will work. Compose the image on tracing paper. This thin paper allows you to combine new imagery with symbols or details from other images you may have made. When the drawing is completed, turn it over onto the printing surface. Rub the back of the paper with a baren or wooden spoon. The charcoal will easily transfer onto the carving surface. This can also be done on an etching press with moderate pressure. After the image is on the woodblock, spray it with acrylic fixative. **SAFETY NOTE: In a well ventilated area, if possible.** This will prevent it from smudging during the carving process.

Carbon paper transfer: Place the drawing or design on a piece of carbon paper, and then place both on the wood. Redraw the linear elements with soft pencil and light pressure. Too much pressure may make indentations in the wood that will print as white lines. With this method you can also create your own drawing or transfer found images to your woodblock. A spray fixative will prevent the lines from distorting on the block during carving.

A drawing created in charcoal or chalk on thin paper will transfer to a board by hand rubbing.

*James Surls, **Untitled**, no date. Woodcut, 48 x 96" (122 x 244 cm). Courtesy the artist.*

Photocopy transfer: A fast and accurate way to transfer a drawing or photograph onto a woodblock is with a photocopy. Photocopy machines can blow 35 mm slides up to a large format. These images can be further increased in size with other photocopying equipment. The copy machine itself has become a wonderful drawing tool. Once copied papers can be fed into the machine over and over again to layer images. These images can be transferred with lacquer thinner directly onto the wood. **SAFETY NOTE: Active ventilation and a respirator are needed with this solvent.** The paper image should be placed face down on the block and taped along the top edge to hold it in place during the process. The lacquer thinner is applied with a wide brush to the wood and then the paper is burnished in place with a wooden spoon or baren. Because the solvent evaporates quickly, only small areas should be worked at a time, but extremely good reproduction will occur. This transfer process can also be done directly onto areas of a printing paper to create multiple techniques on the same print. The freedom to appropriate and manipulate images in the photocopy machine and to increase their scale makes this an exciting process for the contemporary artist.

*Susan Mackin Dolan, **Clear Cut**, 1989. Woodblock print, 12 x 16"*
(30 x 41 cm). Courtesy the artist.

Leni Fried, **World Travellers III***, 1984. Collagraph, 17 x 17" (43 x 43 cm). Courtesy Rugg Road Paper and Prints.*
Photo: Kay Canavino.

collagraph

6

There are two basic ways to produce a collagraph print. You can prepare the collagraph plate as you would any relief print, inking only the highest areas, or you can force ink into the recessed areas and remove it from the high spots, as you would in intaglio processes. Either way, collagraph, which means, literally, "glue writing," yields exciting and often unexpected results.

The collage relief print, in which high areas are inked, relies for its effect on the textural qualities of the various materials that make up its surface. The process for making a plate is usually additive. You can glue, staple, sew, tape and nail low relief objects to masonite, plywood or even linoleum. You can also simply ink up found objects such as crushed cans, leaves and pieces of lace and place them on a printing plate.

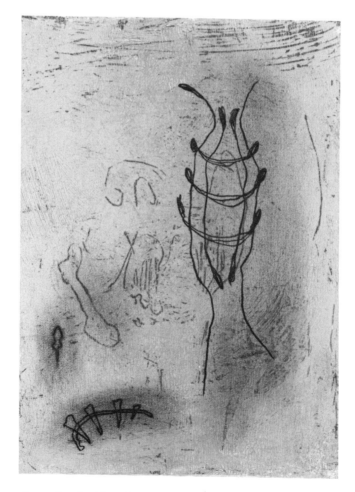

*Susan Laufer, **Transformation Series #3**, 1989. Collagraph, relief and line engraving, 19 x 14" (48 x 36 cm). Courtesy Pace Editions.*

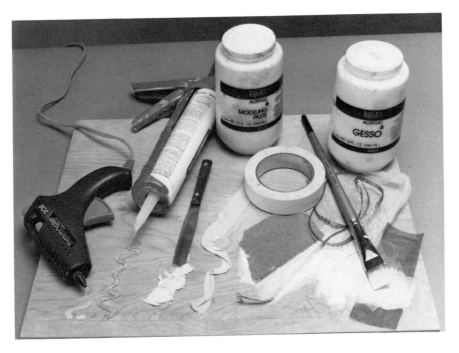

Hot glue, silicone sealer, acrylic gels, tape, paper and screening can be used to make collagraph plates.

Two plates (in the middle of the photograph) and the collagraph prints they produced. The light-colored plate is made from acrylic modeling paste. Fine cloth was used to create the darker plate. The finished plates have been sealed with dilute polyurethane to harden them before inking and printing. Both prints reveal the delicate textures of their materials.

When ink is rolled over this collection of materials, an often surprising print appears. What you see as the collage is not always what you get as a print. The uninked areas of the collage elements often add texture to the image by appearing as embossing.

The term collagraph is most often applied to a collage plate that is printed by the intaglio method of inking. When printed on an etching press, collagraphs produce tonal effects that would not be present if the collage were printed with relief inking. A combination of both collagraph and relief inking procedures reveals a wide range of aspects of the collage elements.

CONSTRUCTING THE PLATE

Any rigid material can serve as a base for your collage as long as it can withstand the inking and printing process. Heavy cardboard, acid free mat board, masonite, plywood or linoleum work well. Liquid glue can be used as a texturing agent or an adhesive, and can be used to draw lines. Gesso, applied thickly, creates fluid lines. When it is dry, it can be carved into far sharper details. Acrylic gel medium works well as an adhesive for paper and cloth elements. It will also hold in place small metal objects like watch parts and washers as well as sand and glitter. You can also combine carved elements with collage elements on a wood or linoleum plate to add more diversity to the image. Collage elements should be kept to within 1/16-inch in height to prevent problems during printing. Elements higher than this might cause the paper to tear or cut into the blankets on the press. Before the collage is ready to print, the surface must be sealed to prevent deterioration during the inking. Two light applications of acrylic gel should be enough. Be careful not to apply the sealer too heavily. You don't want to obscure all of the beautiful textures you just spent time creating on the plate.

INKING AND PRINTING

The inking and printing processes you choose will probably depend upon the look you want for your print. As we've said, collagraph plates can be printed relief or intaglio style. They can also be printed in both styles on the same print using contrasting inks to reveal all of the effects of the plate.

Daubers are easily made by rolling felt and binding it with string or tape.

The plate can be inked intaglio style. A dauber forces ink into the recessed areas.

If the plate is to be printed with the relief inking method, soft inks and soft rollers will force ink deep into the surface of the plate, revealing more of the image when printed. Water-based inks are fine to use for printing collagraphs, though care must be taken to prevent distortion of the plate. If water comes in contact with the collage elements they may swell and change the image. This often happens when the plates are being cleaned. Oil-based inks and their solvents, although posing safety and cleanup difficulties, are less likely to cause this problem.

Printing the collagraph intaglio style involves forcing the ink into the deepest recesses of the plate. These are the areas that you want to print. Excess ink is wiped off the high spots. Ink can be spread over the plate with a rectangular piece of cardboard or mat board cut to two or three inches in length. This method works well if the collage elements are not raised too high off the surface of the plate. Working over the surface several times forces the ink into the plate. Tarlatan, starched cheesecloth or other open weave cloths or hard paper towels are then used to wipe the highest surfaces of the plate clean before printing. If the collage elements are too high for this type of action, ink can be forced into the plate with a dauber. Daubers are made from small rolls of felt six to eight inches wide. The felt should be rolled into a cylinder

Using a dauber to ink a plate intaglio style reveals the negative areas of the plate. On the left is the printed image of the plate pictured on the right.

The plate can also be inked relief style. On the left is the printed image of the plate pictured on the right. This method will show the raised areas of the plate.

long enough to be easy to hold. Wrapped tightly with string or tape, the inked dauber is pounded against the surface of the plate. This forces ink into the recesses. Again, the higher surfaces are wiped clean before the plate is ready to print.

Collagraph plates inked intaglio style can also be inked relief style in a contrasting color. This requires the use of inks with two different viscosities, or thicknesses. Relief inking, when combined with intaglio inking, requires an oil-based ink that has more oil in it than the intaglio ink. The two different consistencies of ink repel each other, allowing them to print simultaneously the high and the low spots on the plate.

PAPER

Plates with relatively low relief, inked with the relief inking method, can be printed on lightweight paper if they are carefully rubbed with a wooden spoon or baren. To protect the thin paper from being torn by the collage elements, a second sheet of heavier weight paper should be laid on top of the first sheet as a barrier or cushion.

Thick paper is essential for printing high-relief collagraphs. The

*The artist pressed collage elements onto an inked piece of broken Plexiglas. She then printed the plate. Melissa Johnson, **Monoprint**, 1988. Monotype made from negative collagraph, 20 x 16" (51 x 41 cm). Courtesy the artist.*

This image is made from masking tape attached to a Plexiglas plate. It has been printed three different ways: intaglio, relief and using freehand brushstrokes to tone the plate.

dimensional surface of the plate causes the paper to stretch and be pulled during printing. Heavy weight watercolor paper, dampened, works best for prints with high relief elements like thick cardboard or metal objects. Regular weight printmaking paper will work on plates where the texture and image are made from lower-relief elements like tape, cloth and other papers. The papers should always be dampened before printing to give them the flexibility they need to stretch over the objects. Also, a few sheets of newsprint should be placed on top of the printing paper before it is run through the press just in case the objects do tear through the paper and cut or stain the felt blankets of the press. You might also try running the plate through the press several times, gradually increasing the pressure. This will allow the paper more time to stretch gradually over the relief elements.

The finished print should be dried between blotters under less pressure than you would normally use. Part of the beauty of a collagraph print is its

Archie Rand and Jon Cone are shown here working on an editioned print titled **Assimilation**. *The plate is assembled from found objects — in this case, potatoes. They have cut, carved and fitted together many pounds of potatoes which will then be inked and printed by hand rubbing. Courtesy Cone Editions Press.*

embossed surface. Drying the print under too much pressure will flatten some of the embossing.

CLEANING THE PLATE

A collagraph plate can often be difficult to clean because of its dimensional surface. If printing was done with water-based inks, care should be taken during cleaning to prevent the water from coming in contact with the collage materials, causing them to swell and distort the plate. If oil-based inks were used, it might be necessary to flush the plate with solvents several times to remove all of the ink. **SAFETY NOTE: Use excess solvents in this manner only in an area with active ventilation. Wear gloves.**

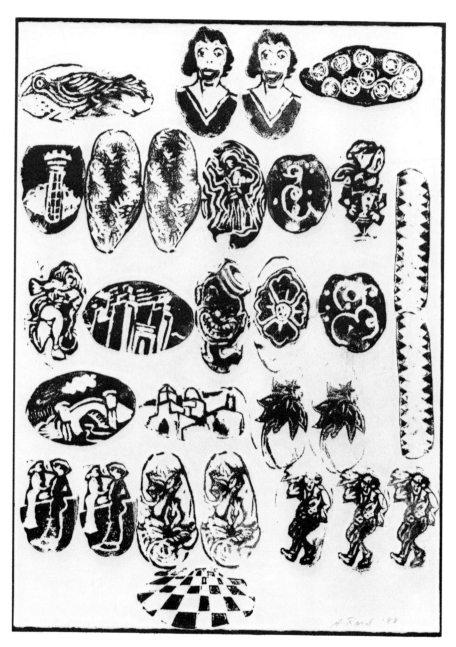

*Archie Rand, **Story**, 1988. Potato print, 26 x 20" (66 x 51 cm). Courtesy Cone Editions Press.*

*Agusta Agustsson, **Endangered Polar Bear**, 1980. Silkscreen, 38 x 42" (97 x 107 cm). Courtesy The Graphics Workshop, Boston. Photo: Willa Heider.*

S ilkscreen printing, also called serigraphy (Latin for "silk writing"), is neither a relief printmaking process (such as cardboard, linoleum, woodblock and collagraph), nor necessarily a way to create one-of-a-kind prints (such as monotype). Silkscreen printing is based on the principle of the stencil. In stenciling, ink is applied through a sturdy cutout shape onto a surface below. In silkscreen printmaking, stencils, or shapes made with a material thick enough to fill the fine holes of a "silk screen," block the ink in some areas. The ink moves through the screen in the unblocked areas and prints onto paper or another surface placed below the screen.

Silkscreen printmaking is a relatively new process, but stenciling, its predecessor, has a long history. The

*Frank Stella, **La Penna di Hu**, 1988. Relief, etching, woodcut, screenprint, stencil, 55 ½ x 66" (141 x 168 cm), edition of 50. Printed and published by Tyler Graphics Ltd. Copyright Frank Stella/Tyler Graphics, 1988.*

earliest examples of stencil print-making come from prehistoric times. Artists' hands were reproduced by a primitive spraying technique that left their silhouettes on the walls of caves in France and Spain. Natural earth pigments were sprayed around the edge of the fingers with a blow gun made from a hollow reed. The pigment was prob-ably stored in the artist's mouth. The negative shape of the hand was created and remains today as a testament to the innate creativity of the human species. Positive images of hands were also found. These were made by placing the hand in the wet pigment and then slapping it against the wall. These are the earliest examples of stamping techniques.

The Japanese mastered the stenciling technique centuries ago and used it to create elaborate textile designs. Complicated stencils were cut into two layers of thin, waterproof paper. Intricate and freestanding parts of the image were held in place by fine threads or strands of human hair. These threads were laminated between the two layers of paper to

Hall of Bulls, *left wall, Lascaux, ca. 15,000-13,000 BC. Dordogne, France. Courtesy SPADEM, Paris.*

hold them in place. The stencils were placed on the cloth. Dye or watercolor was applied with a stiff, short-bristled brush by pounding.

Fifteenth century European playing cards, although printed with woodblocks, were colored with stencils. Textiles and wallpaper were printed by this simple hand process and with the use of stamps. Oiled paper, similar to modern oak tag, and thin metal were cut by early Americans to put patterns on walls, floors, furniture and textiles, and to create artworks.

Silkscreen printing in a form similar to what we know today was patented in England in 1907. Since then, its applications have become universal. We use it to create giant advertising billboards and the circuitry for our smallest computers. It is used to make glaze patterns on fine dinnerware and the red and white label on a Coke can. The Pop artists of the 1960s brought silkscreen into the world of fine art printmaking as a method of reproducing photographic images and producing flat areas of color.

The modern silkscreen process is a straightforward and simple way to accomplish multicolor printmaking. It is relatively inexpensive and requires little equipment in comparison to other techniques. A silk screen is made from silk, polyester or nylon cloth stretched over a strong wooden frame. This frame is usually attached by hinges to a baseboard slightly larger than the frame. The paper or cloth printing surface is placed on the baseboard, the frame lowered, and the ink forced through the screen with a broad rubber- or plastic-edged board, known as a squeegee. Images are created on the screen with simple stencils or by drawing with a thick material. Photographic processes can also be used to create complicated, crisp images and painterly effects. Both water- and oil-based inks can be used to create subtle or bold images. Unlike other printing methods, the silkscreened image is not reversed when printed but appears in the same direction as the original drawing.

Andy Warhol, **Marilyn,** *1967. Silkscreen, 36 x 36" (91 x 91 cm). Private collection.*

Intricate stencils made from treated mulberry paper were used to create pattern on Japanese textiles. Here you can see the results when ink is forced through the openings in a delicate stencil with a stiff brush.

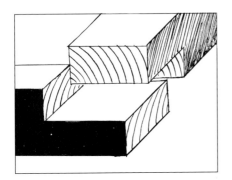

A lap joint.

BASIC COMPONENTS

The screen

The screen has three parts: the frame that holds the cloth, the cloth and a baseboard.

The frame: The frame is made of kiln-dried wood joined at the corners. The construction of the corner should be strong to prevent the screen from distorting. Lap joints make a strong and dependable corner. The size of the frame should be at least three inches larger in all dimensions than the squeegee you will be using, to allow easy printing. Frames should be constructed of wood at least two inches by two inches thick, and thicker for large frames. When constructing your frame, keep in mind that a small frame is less comfortable to work with than a larger one. Frames that measure 25 x 33" (64 x 84 cm) on the inside are quite versatile. They will fit standard 22 x 30" (56 x 76 cm) papers and can be masked off for smaller sheets. Temporary frames can be made from commercial canvas stretchers used for paintings. The corners must be reinforced with screws to keep them rigid.

The cloth: The frame should be covered with cloth made from silk, polyester, nylon or dacron. Silk is a natural fiber, every thread of which is composed of many finer filaments. This characteristic makes it easy for stencils to be attached to it and for dry and liquid masking media to become trapped in its surface. The other fabrics mentioned are synthetics. Some are multifilamented, like silk, and others are monofilament. Your choice of material will depend to some degree upon the technique and solvent that you will be using.

The weight and fineness of the cloth will also determine the look of the image that you print. Finer cloth will produce greater detail. Coarser cloth will allow more ink through and produce dense color areas. Silk and multifilament polyester are sold according to weight. An "X" indicates standard weight cloth; "XX" indicates heavy weight cloth. Cloth is also sold according to the fineness of the weave. "6X" and "6XX" indi-

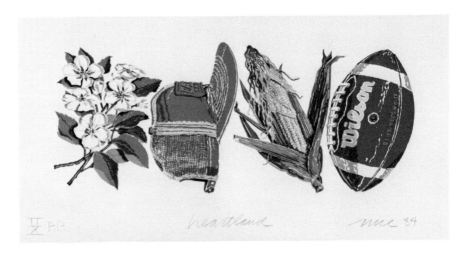

*Don Nice, **Heartland**, 1984. Silkscreen print, courtesy Stewart & Stewart.*

Hinges of this type allow screens to be changed easily without affecting the registration of the image.

cate coarse weave in regular and heavy weight cloth. "20X" and "20XX" indicate fine weave in both weights. For general usage, "12XX" is good. These materials are available at silkscreen supply stores around the country. The staff of these stores will always help you choose the appropriate cloth for your project.

Silk is the finest, most versatile material available for many techniques. It is also the most expensive. It is very tough and can be reused many times. Paper stencils adhere well to it. Liquid masking materials like tusche can be used easily on it. Crayons can be used to create sensitive drawing effects. It can also be used for indirect photographic techniques. It is unaffected by most solvents but cannot be used with strong acids or alkalis. It is therefore not suitable for direct photographic processes that require bleach.

Polyester fabrics are versatile and long lasting. They can be used with all techniques and all types of solvents. They come monofilamented and multifilamented. Multifilamented polyester takes tusche and crayon drawing with great detail.

When ordering fabric, allow two or three extra inches beyond the dimension of the frame on all sides. For a 25 x 33" frame, purchase 29 x 37" cloth. Because of its many applications, silkscreen cloth comes in widths ranging from forty inches to six feet.

The baseboard: The baseboard should be smooth, and larger than the frame by several inches in all directions. Formica or tile board glued to a ½" piece of plywood makes an excellent surface. The frame is hinged to it. Hinging helps to ensure accurate registration when printing. If your work space allows, the frame can be hinged directly to your table. Hinges with removable pins make changing the screen easy. There are also special hinges available at silkscreen supply stores designed for this purpose. They are clamp hinges and attach to the frame with a wing nut. They are very versatile and allow for the use of many different-sized frames.

Alignment blocks prevent the frame from moving from side to side during printing. They are placed at the end of the frame opposite the hinges. Two small pieces of wood can be screwed into the baseboard next to the frame when it is in the down position. They can be unscrewed and moved again when a new frame is used.

The squeegee

The squeegee is the tool used to spread the ink across the surface of the screen and push it through the screen onto the printing surface. It consists of a rubber or plastic blade mounted in a wooden handle. It must be wide enough to cover the image with a few inches to spare. It must also be about two inches smaller than the inside measurement of the frame in order to move freely during printing. The blade is the critical part of the squeegee. Its flexibility and shape will help determine the results of the printing. Many different blades are available for specific projects.

For printing flat work, a square-edged blade is most commonly used. Round-edged squeegees are used when a thick application of ink is needed. This is usually in textile printing.

The composition of the squeegee is also important. Rubber and polyurethane blades are long lasting and seldom need resharpening. They can be used with oil- or water-based inks and solvents. Neoprene squeegees should only be used with oil-based inks. They become dry and brittle if washed in soap and water. They also require occasional resharpening.

You can buy a squeegee sharpener or make one yourself. It should be longer than your squeegee. It consists of two pieces of wood joined at a right angle. One piece is covered with garnet paper or fine sandpaper. Pull the squeegee along the abrasive paper while keeping it vertical and parallel to the other board. Sanding will remove small nicks or dents in the blade. If the dent is deep, the edge of the squeegee can be cut off with a sharp knife and then re-sanded. A sharp edge is essential for clear and even printing.

Leo Byrnes, **The Rain Forest — Endangered***, 1988. Silkscreen, 26 x 21"* *(66 x 53 cm). Courtesy The Graphics Workshop, Boston.*

Leo Byrnes, **Gila Monster, Endangered**, 1989. Silkscreen, 37 x 26" (94 x 66 cm). Courtesy The Graphics Workshop, Boston.

Sondra Freckelton, **Blue Chenille**, 1985. Screenprint, 24 x 33" (61 x 83 cm). Courtesy Stewart & Stewart.

Jane E. Goldman, **Mid-Summer Light**, 1987. Screenprint, 33 x 24" (84 x 61 cm). Courtesy Stewart & Stewart.

Lisa Houck, **Darters, Endangered**, 1988. Silkscreen, 39 x 19⅝" (99 x 50 cm). Courtesy The Graphics Workshop, Boston.

*Richard Treaster, **Vermeer and Times**, 1984. Screenprint, 49 x 36" (124 x 91 cm). Courtesy Stewart & Stewart.*

CONSTRUCTING THE SCREEN

The most important factor in good printing is the tightness of the cloth on the frame. If the cloth is loose, it will cause a blurred image and will make registration difficult. Silk should be hand washed and rinsed to remove sizing. Polyester requires no pretreatment. Nylon may need to be stretched and then restretched to get proper tension.

Some premade silkscreen frames and frame stock have a groove cut in the bottom of the frame. When the cloth has been placed across the frame, a cord is hammered into the groove to tighten the fabric. This simple method can produce a tightly stretched surface with relatively little effort. If you want to change the screen, all you have to do is pull out the cord and remove the cloth.

Stapling the fabric

A special tape is used when stapling the fabric onto the frame. This strong tape is placed over the cloth as it rests on the frame and is attached at the same time. This tape adds thickness to the cloth and helps hold the staples in place without tearing the fine fabric. It is also use-

1

Lay the cloth tape over the silkscreen and begin stapling at the center of the screen, working toward the edges.

ful when the screen is to be replaced. Its strength allows you simply to pull on it and remove all the staples at one time without damaging the screen.

Lay the fabric over the frame, leaving an extra two inches on all sides. Make sure that the vertical threads of the cloth are parallel to the sides of the frame. Lay the tape over the fabric and attach tape and fabric to the frame along one edge. Staple the fabric with several staples in the middle of the frame, spaced one inch apart. Staple at an angle rather than parallel to the edge to prevent the fabric from ripping. Then pull the cloth tightly across the frame and staple it to the middle

2

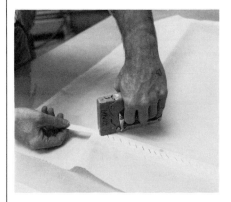

Stapling at an angle prevents the cloth from tearing. SAFETY NOTE: Use staple guns with extreme care.

of the other side with several staples spaced one inch apart. Repeat this for the other two sides. Pull and staple each side in rotation, working out from the center of each side. A pair of stretching pliers can be used to put additional tension into the process. Then go back again, placing additional staples between the first staples, tightening as you work. When the fabric is tightly drawn, take a hammer and pound the staples flush with the frame.

Taping the screen

Brown paper tape moistened with water should be applied to the inside and outside of the frame.

3

Hammer the staples to reinforce them.

4

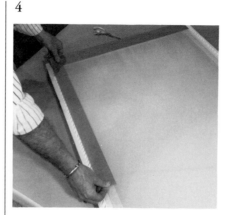

Paper tape should cover the staples and extend ¾" (2 cm) onto the cloth.

5

On the inside of the screen, the tape should cover the frame and extend 1 ½" (4 cm) onto the cloth. An extra width of tape should be placed at the end where the ink and squeegee rest.

6

Spring loaded legs automatically lift the screen between printings.

This prevents ink from collecting between the cloth and the sides of the frame. It also serves to isolate the image in the center of the frame.

Ordinary three-inch-wide brown paper tape with a water-soluble glue backing can be placed around the inside of the frame next to the wood. Attach a second piece of tape, folded in half lengthwise, to the wooden frame and the taped screen. On the back of the frame, tape should be placed from the outside edge of the wood, covering the staples or cording. A second piece of tape should overlap the first and go to within ½" of the inside edge of the tape on the reverse side.

After the tape has dried, it should be coated with two layers of shellac or lacquer on both sides of the screen. This seals the tape and prevents water or ink from absorbing into it. **SAFETY NOTE: Active ventilation should be available when using shellac or lacquer. Wear a respirator and gloves. Refer to solvents caution on page 112.**

A one by one inch board four to six inches long should be screwed to the side of the frame. This serves as a leg to prop up the screen between printings. It keeps the inked screen from depositing ink on the baseboard and then onto the back of the next print. Commercially available legs with spring attachments are also available.

Preparing the screen

After stretching, screens must be given a small amount of texture. This texture helps the stencils adhere to the surface. This can easily be done by scrubbing the screen with powdered cleanser, pumice or No. 400 carborundum, an industrial polishing medium. A nylon scrub brush or fingernail brush can be used to work the abrasive into the screen. Rinse thoroughly with water to remove any particles. This washing process also causes the fabric to shrink and tighten further on the frame.

REGISTRATION

Attached to the baseboard will be some system for allowing you to position a sheet of paper for printing. Prints with several colors require precise positioning for accurate alignment. The system you select will depend on the type and thickness of the printing surface you're using. Cloth, paper, cardboard and wood are each handled differently. The method you choose will also depend on the edge of that surface. A deckled or irregular edge will require special consideration. In all systems you will need three regis-

tration guides. Two will be at the bottom edge and one will be halfway up one of the sides. The guides will change with each new print series, so they should be attached in a temporary way. In most cases, the printing paper must be cut with squared corners to allow for precise registration. This is especially important when you are producing multicolored prints which require several registrations.

Register strips

For most prints, simple register strips ¾" x 2" in length work well. They are made of thin cardboard, plastic or heavy weight paper. They are attached to the baseboard by a temporary bond such as spray adhesive or water-soluble glue. Two are placed at the bottom of the printing paper and one is halfway up its side. The paper is butted up against these strips for perfect registration.

T Registration

This very simple system works well for papers with irregular edges, and is especially suited for handmade papers. A pencil line is drawn on three registration strips positioned on the baseboard as described above.

This line is also drawn on the board itself. A continuation of this pencil line is drawn on the front side of the printing paper. These lines are visually realigned each time you print a new color.

Metal button registration

This registration system works well for large prints. Metal buttons (commercially available) are taped to the board or table outside of the frame. Cardboard tabs with a hole in each are attached to the back of the printing paper. To register the print, simply fit the hole in the tab onto the button.

INKS

Water- and oil-based inks can be used for silkscreen printing. Many of the new water-based inks produce results almost identical to oil-based inks, without the need for organic solvents. These newer inks have retardants added to them to slow their drying time. The problem of fast drying used to be a drawback of water-based inks, and made oil-based inks the favorite of screen printers. For teaching situations, where safety and easy cleanup are especially important, the new water-based inks are ideal.

Oil-based inks also have some attractive qualities. They are available with matte or gloss surfaces and metallic or fluorescent colors. They can be formulated to print on paper, cloth, metal, glass or ceramics. Like other inks, they require some modification before you can print with them. Extenders, such as transparent base, make the ink more fluid without diluting the color. Solvents thin the ink. As a general rule, adding ten percent of transparent base to any ink will make it pass through the screen more easily and reduce clogging. Some colors — black and dark blue, for example — can be thinned to a greater extent without affecting their opacity. Properly prepared ink should be the consistency of heavy cream, falling freely from the stirring stick when it is lifted.

Silkscreen printing requires the use of more ink than many of the other processes described in this book. When you have blended the color you require, be sure to make enough to print your whole project. Excess ink can be stored in metal cans with plastic lids for future projects. One-pound coffee cans or small cat food cans with plastic lids work well for storing oil-based inks.

Felice Regan, **Koala Bear***, no date. Silkscreen, 30 x 24" (76 x 61 cm). Courtesy The Graphics Workshop, Boston.*

Plastic containers do not work well because they dissolve over a period of time. Paper cups work well for mixing small quantities of ink but should not be used for storage.

When mixing oil-based inks there are several things to consider. Inks produced by some manufacturers are not always compatible with inks produced by other manufacturers. Some inks contain polyurethane. Some contain vinyl and some are rubber-based. Check the manufacturer's specifications and make small test samples before committing yourself to a big project. **As with any oil-based product, be careful when using these inks. Make sure there is adequate ventilation, and that your skin is protected from contact with the ink.**

SOLVENTS

The one drawback to silkscreen printing for many artists and teachers is the great many solvents used in the process. This seems an unavoidable situation if oil-based inks and photographic processes are used. If you must use these processes, remember that many techniques can be done using simple, multipurpose solvents. With the proper care and adequate ventilation, this does not have to be an unhealthy activity.

Nonetheless, certain rules should be followed when working with or around solvents.

1. **Don't smoke or work with a flame in the same room.**
2. **Avoid using more than one solvent at a time in the same room. The combined effect of several solvents together can be dangerous.**
3. **Store all solvents in metal containers and when possible store these in a ventilated metal storage cabinet.**
4. **Use solvent-resistant protective hand cream or wear rubber gloves.**
5. **Work in a well-ventilated area.**
6. **If necessary, wear a facial respirator with a filter cartridge rated for the removal of aromatic and chlorinated hydrocarbons.**
7. **Dispose of all used materials and empty containers at the end of the day in a safe and responsible manner. Never pour excess solvents down the drain. Treat them as hazardous waste.**

TECHNIQUES

There are several manuals on silkscreen printing that detail the many techniques available with this process. The following brief explanation will help you choose a process suitable to your image-making and your studio facilities.

Stencils

In any kind of silkscreen printing, a stencil of one material or another determines the image area and controls where the ink is placed. Images cut from thin, opaque paper can be attached to the underside of the screen, held there simply by the ink used to print the image. No additional adhesives are needed, and no solvents are required to remove it. Special effects can be created by exposing torn edges on shapes or by using thin papers that will allow a certain amount of ink to pass through them to create shadowed areas. Because these stencils are impermanent, they cannot be used for great numbers of identical prints, but the simplicity of this technique and the fact that it uses inexpensive materials makes it a good place to start your exploration of the process.

Simple stencils for silkscreening can be cut from lightweight paper using a mat knife.

The stencil is placed beneath the frame. Ink is distributed across the top of the frame using a palette knife.

The ink is pulled across the screen with a squeegee.

Ink holds the stencil in place after the first print is pulled.

A more permanent stencil can be cut from water-soluble or lacquer-soluble film. These films are dissolved by their solvents and melted onto the underside of the screen. They will remain in place without shifting or distorting until they are removed by a solvent. Stencil cutting knives can be purchased and used to create clean, detailed images on the films. The films are made of two layers. The lacquer-like layer is attached to a thicker plastic or paper layer that acts as a support during the cutting of the stencil. This layer is not cut during the process. The lacquer layer is cut and the shapes removed. This material is available in small sheets or large rolls at all silkscreen suppliers.

Film stencils are transparent and can be laid over your drawing during the cutting process. Care must be taken to cut only the lacquer layer of the film and not the backing layer or your drawing. With a little practice this becomes easier.

The final stencil is positioned under your screen. The screen is lowered to rest on it and a solvent (either water and acetic acid or lacquer thinner) is used to adhere it to the screen.

Freehand drawing

Oil pastels, lithographic crayons and pencils, wax crayons and lithographic tusche can be used to draw directly onto the silkscreen. This freehand method of making an image is spontaneous and direct and will create an image quite different from those made with a cut stencil.

With this process, an image is drawn directly onto the screen with a turpentine-soluble, waxy medium. The screen is then covered with a water-soluble block-out medium. Hide glue, available at hardware and art supply stores, is applied with a small squeegee or stiff cardboard. After it dries, the drawing is washed out of the screen with the solvent. The open spaces are now the stencil for the positive image on your print.

Hide glue can also be used as a drawing tool to create a negative area in an image. It can be used in a lettering pen, applied with stamps or found objects or brushed onto the screen. When it dries, the screen is ready to print with oil-based inks. When the printing is complete, the glue is removed from the screen with warm water.

Photographic techniques

Photographic techniques are used to create stencils with photosensitive materials. Some require darkroom processing. Others can be done in subdued lighting with little or no equipment. Some are done on films that are attached to the screen afterwards. Others are created directly on the screen. All can create crisp stencils of great detail. All rely on the creativity of the artist, and not the process, to create beautiful prints.

A silkscreen coated with a light-sensitive emulsion is placed on a vacuum table with a photographic positive image of the artwork. Courtesy Preston Graphics.

The screen is exposed to the strong light of an arc lamp.

The emulsion hardens with exposure to light and is washed away in the unexposed areas to reveal the image.

A Filbar motorized press speeds production in the Preston Graphics studio.

An electric dryer dries each color in 35 seconds.

Artist James Rosenquist collaborates with Ken Tyler and his assistant at the Tyler Graphics studio. Ken Tyler has built custom-designed presses to accommodate artists' desires to produce large-scale images. Courtesy Tyler Graphics Ltd.

The two most important items in a good print studio are light and ventilation. Add a wall to view your prints on, a strong work table, access to water and you're in business.

Relief printmaking without a press requires little else. You will need places to store clean paper and finished prints, your inks and solvents and your tools. If you are doing editioned printing, you will need a drying rack to hold the wet prints until the ink dries. If you add a press to your studio, it will need a strong table to sit on.

HEALTH CONCERNS

Of critical concern to artists today is health and safety in the studio. For generations these issues were not stressed. With the acknowledgment of the world's fragile ecology and our awareness of the danger of many solvents to our bodies, artists have petitioned suppliers for information on the safety of their products. Some have responded with labels that list harmful ingredients in their products. Others have not responded. There are general improvements that we can make in our studios to show our concern for ourselves and the environment.

One of the simplest ways to prevent personal contamination in the studio is good, practical hygiene. **SAFETY NOTE: Don't eat or drink in there!** Wear rubber gloves when working with solvents and inks, and wash your hands before you leave the studio. These are obvious but simple ways to protect yourself.

Solvents used in the studio are absorbed into our bodies two ways: through the skin and through our lungs. Barrier cream rubbed onto the hands helps prevent absorption of chemicals. It is available through most art, photography and printmaking supply stores. Rubber gloves will also prevent skin contact with solvents. Good ventilation can help to reduce the amount of solvents in the air you breathe.

VENTILATION

The importance of good ventilation cannot be over-stressed. Some solvents absorbed through the lungs are quickly passed out of the body. Some are stored in the lungs and liver and are known to cause cancer in these organs. Strong exhaust fans can take fumes from the room and help to reduce these risks.

Fans are rated according to the percentage of air that they are able to move. When designing or improving a studio it is important to consult a ventilation specialist to make sure that you are using the right equipment. Usually you will need a much larger exhaust system than you anticipated. Aside from a general exhaust system, you may also need a local system to take high concentrations of fumes from your cleanup and solvent areas. A little research could be very beneficial to your health. (Please note the excellent book, *Ventilation*, by Clark, Cutter and McGrane in the bibliography at the end of this book.)

LIGHT

Natural light is wonderful to work in. It strengthens color relationships and enhances subtleties. If a skylight is feasible in your studio, install one. Large, north-facing windows are your next choice. Any windows are of great value and can be opened in good weather to increase ventilation.

Fluorescent lights are better to work under than incandescent light bulbs. Light bulbs produce a yellow-colored light that will greatly distort color relationships in your work. Many different light bulbs are available for fluorescent light fixtures. Choose one that is balanced for daylight. You may wish to supplement this system with a few incandescent spotlights to highlight a viewing wall or cleanup area.

VIEWING WALLS

There is nothing more informative than being able to step back from your print and see it hanging on a wall. You can instantly see if the borders are straight and the ink dense enough. A print laid flat on a table looks very dif-

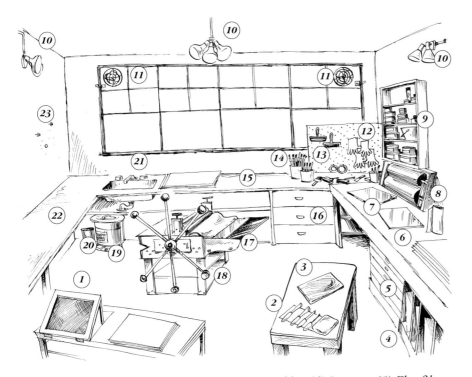

(1) Silk screen. (2) Carving tools. (3) Carving table. (4) Storage. (5) Flat files. (6) Clean area. (7) Glass palettes. (8) Rollers. (9) Ink storage. (10) Lights. (11) Fans. (12) Gloves. (13) Brayers. (14) Brushes. (15) Inking area. (16) General tool storage. (17) Press. (18) Shelves for paper. (19) Combustible waste disposal can. (20) Old solvent disposal container. (21) Sink. (22) Wet paper area. (23) Wall space for viewing prints.

ferent from one tacked up on a wall. You can never have enough viewing space, so plan generously.

The easiest way to put a print up for temporary inspection is with push pins. Pressed through the corners of the print and into a soft wall surface, they can be changed in a matter of seconds. Homosote is the best surface to use for covering your walls. It is made from paper fiber, is easy to pin into, and can be painted. It is easy to install with regular nails or sheetrock screws. It can be installed over an existing wall or a wall can be made of it alone. Harder materials like sheetrock or plywood will work, but it is harder to force the push pins into these. Whatever you choose to build it from, a viewing wall is essential for analyzing the quality of your work.

WORK TABLES

Work tables in a relief print studio should be strong, durable and heavy. Lightweight tables will move around the room as you carve on a large block of wood. They will also be noisy if you are working on your block with a chisel and mallet. The table should be constructed with shelves beneath it for the storage of flat work. A solidly constructed wooden table with a thick wood top will last a lifetime and is worth the effort it takes to make it, or the money it takes to purchase it. This table can also be covered with Formica to give it a smooth and cleanable surface.

The placement of your tables in the studio will determine how easy it will be to work there. If the table is large and placed up against your viewing wall, it will be hard to pin things onto the wall. If the inking area is too close to the printing area, you may get fresh ink on your new prints. Consider the layout of your room carefully for cleanliness and for ease of movement. How many people might be working in the room at one time? Make sure there is enough room for everyone. If the room is comfortable, you will want to spend time there. Making art is not easy. A pleasant, well-thought-out room can encourage you to go back in there and keep trying.

WATER

Having a sink in your studio is very convenient for dampening papers and general cleanup. However, it also presents you with the temptation of dumping solvents down the drain to dispose of them — **which you should never do. Dirty solvents should be stored in metal or glass containers and disposed of according to your town's ordinances.** All communities have drop-off locations for this type of hazardous waste material.

Your local water supply may not be clean enough for your studio needs. Printmaking papers dampened with water containing excess minerals will discolor around the edges. These minerals and other contaminants can be removed with filters. Some water filters can be attached directly to your incoming water line. There are also portable filtration systems that attach to the faucet or can be held over a bottle or jar to allow you to filter small quantities of water. Whichever you choose, it is important to consider your water source and your needs.

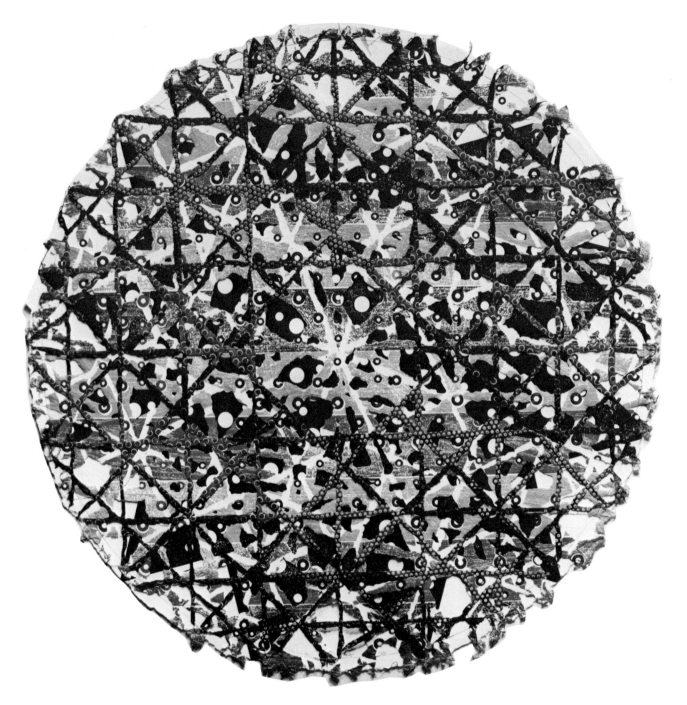

Alan Shields, **Trade Route (Roman)**, *1985. Woodcut, silkscreen, relief, 47" (119 cm) diameter, edition of 20. Courtesy Tyler Graphics Ltd. Copyright Alan Shields/Tyler Graphics Ltd., 1985.*

Papermakers will say that printmaking advanced with the advancements made in papermaking. Printmakers will say that their ever-growing need for new and interesting papers led to advances in papermaking. Whichever is actually the case, your choice of paper is extremely important to the success of your print.

There are really three different products that can be defined as paper. They are Oriental, European and machine-made papers. Each starts with a different raw material and the resulting papers have distinctly different working characteristics. Papers from each of these categories can be used to make beautiful prints and each is worth experimenting with.

ORIENTAL PAPERS

Oriental papers are made from raw plant materials that are grown specifically for papermaking. These thin and pliable papers are well suited for hand rubbed relief prints. They are produced from three specific plants.

The most common fiber in Oriental papers is called kozo. It is a domesticated plant, easily grown, that produces a strong paper with a light tan color. It has been used for lampshades, umbrellas and textiles in Japan and is often dyed to make a rainbow of colored papers. These papers often contain decorative materials like long fibers or added elements like leaves and flowers.

Mitsumata fiber produces a fine-textured paper with a warm reddish tone. This plant is not as easy to grow and these papers are not as common.

Gampi produces a smooth-surfaced, lustrous white paper that appears to glow from within. It is the most beautiful of all the natural fiber papers. It is difficult to grow, but because it is so sought after it is not uncommon on the market, just expensive.

All of these plant fibers are made into a range of papers from thin to thick. Each will affect your print in a different way. Some are made by hand and others are made by machine.

EUROPEAN PAPERS

European papers are made from textiles. Historically they were made from discarded, well-worn clothing — hence the term "rag" paper. The two most common fibers for these papers were linen and cotton, because that is what people made their clothing from. Cotton produces an absorbent, soft paper by comparison to linen, which is usually crisp and hard. Because of their strength, these papers are well suited for processes that put a lot of stress on the sheet, such as etching or collagraph. Fine European papers are generally made by hand, one at a time. These papers can also be made by machine.

MACHINE-MADE PAPERS

Machine-made papers are usually made from trees. Once the tree is harvested and broken down mechanically into chips, the wood is processed with strong chemicals to help separate the fibers. After macerating in a machine called a Hollander beater, this fine pulp is then squirted onto a machine with a rapidly moving web of fabric that produces paper with a strong directional grain.

Machine-made papers have a reputation for being acidic and weak. Our libraries are filled with books made in the nineteenth and twentieth centuries that are falling apart within their bindings. Newsprint is one of these kinds of papers. It is indispensable in the print studio and classroom. It can be used for student projects, for testing a printed image and for general cleanup work, but should not be used for making finished prints that will be sold. There are, however, machine-made papers of fine quality that are buffered with calcium carbonate and often include cotton fiber. These are readily available and modestly priced. Qualified sales people should be able to tell you the characteristics of each paper.

A subcategory of machine-made paper is mold-made paper. This is paper usually made of cotton or of a cotton blend. It is produced on a papermaking machine that has a slow moving fabric web. The resulting papers have less directional grain and more dimensional stability than regular machine-made papers. It is also readily available in art supply stores.

Beyond these there are still two other groups of papers for the printmaker to consider. These are non-woven textiles and artist-made papers.

Many interesting effects can be achieved using non-woven textiles as a printing surface. This "cloth" can be purchased at fabric stores and is used as interfacing material in clothing construction. It is often sold under the trade name of Pelon. It comes in several weights, from gossamer thin to medium. It has a very smooth surface with a slight sheen. It can be used to create veils of color or layers of imagery.

With the recent introduction of hand papermaking into the curriculum of many schools, students and artists have learned to create a wide range of papers for their personal needs. Depending on the machinery available to you, you can make papers that are roughly textured and organically shaped or resemble traditional high quality handmade sheets. They can be subtly or dramatically colored, even multicolored. They can also be unconventionally shaped. All these features can enhance your prints and your love of the process. There are several good books on the market now that describe this process and show examples of contemporary works. Be sure to look for them and give it a try.

A LOOK AT THE PAPERMAKING PROCESS

1

Paint mixers can be used to prepare pre-processed cotton fibers (known as linter) for artist papermaking.

2

A traditional European-style mold and deckle.

3

A simple, durable papermaking mold can be made using a plastic grid as the support system, hardware cloth as an underwire, and a finer wire on the top surface.

4

Pulp is collected on the mold and the mold is shaken to align the fibers.

5

The deckle is removed and the excess water is allowed to drain.

6

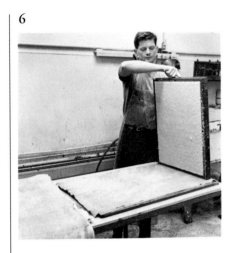

The mold is aligned with the wool blanket.

7

The mold is pressed against the blanket.

8

The freshly-made paper remains on the blanket.

9

Pressing extracts water. The papers are then dried between blotters.

FORMING AND LAYERING MULTICOLORED PAPERS

Papermakers at Tyler Graphics dip a frame on which string has been stretched into the paper pulp.

The frame is laid onto another newly-formed round sheet of paper to form a patterned layer.

With the frame removed, the layers can be pressed together…

…to form a multicolored sheet. Photo series courtesy Tyler Graphics Ltd.

Pulp can be sprayed onto a screen to form decoration or texture. Here paper is being made for artist Alan Shields' **Uncle Ferdinand's Route** *print at Tyler Graphics. Courtesy Tyler Graphics Ltd.*

Decorative pulps can be put into squeeze bottles to form color areas …

...that can then be printed on.
Courtesy Tyler Graphics Ltd.

Newly formed, shaped papers of
different colors can be layered together
to form patterned sheets. Courtesy
Tyler Graphics Ltd.

*Alan Shields stitches together layers of papers for his three-layered print **Milan Fog**. Courtesy Tyler Graphics Ltd.*

*Alan Shields, **Milan Fog**, 1984. Woodcut, etching, aquatint, stitching, collage, 39¾ x 32" (101 x 81 cm). Printed and published by Tyler Graphics Ltd. Copyright Alan Shields/Tyler Graphics Ltd., 1984.*

A THREE-DIMENSIONAL PRINT

1

Artist Eric Avery combines printmaking and papermaking to make three-dimensional prints. Using traditional woodcarving tools, he creates his image on the back of a large wooden tray.

2

The finished carving is then sealed to prevent the wood from absorbing water during the papermaking process.

3

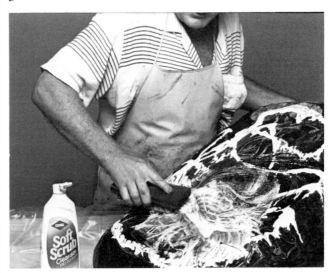

During editioning, an abrasive is used to clean ink off the wood between printings and to insure that paper pulp will not stick to the block.

4

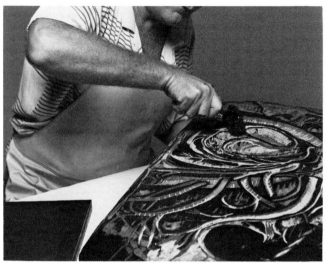

The carving is inked with oil-based ink.

5

Colored paper pulps are fitted together on the inked plate.

6

A final layer of white pulp is pressed by hand with a sponge.

7

The paper is dried on the wooden tray using electric fans.

When the cast paper is removed from the wooden form, it reveals its printed interior. Eric Avery, **Organ Bowl***, 1990. Cast paper woodblock print, 19 x 35 ½ x 3 ½" (48 x 90 x 9 cm). Courtesy the artist. Photo series by Tim Summa, Southwest Craft Center, San Antonio, Texas.*

a gallery of prints from many cultures

a gallery of prints
from many cultures

Rafael Tufino,
Cortador de Cana
(Cane Cutter),
1951-52.
Linocut on paper,
11 ½ x 18 ½"
(29 x 47 cm).
Museum of
History,
Anthropology
and Art of the
University of
Puerto Rico.
Photograph:
John Betancourt,
San Juan.

*Elizabeth Catlett, **Sharecropper**, 1970. Linoleum cut on paper, 17 ¹³⁄₁₆ x 16 ¹⁵⁄₁₆" (45 x 43 cm). National Museum of American Art, Smithsonian Institution, Washington, DC.*

*Emma Amos, **Horizons**, 1968. Relief etching and serigraph, 15 ½ x 15" (39 x 38 cm). Copyright Gulf and Western Ind.*

*Jacob Lawrence, **Underground Railroad, Fording a Stream**, 1948. Woodcut, 9 x 14" (23 x 36 cm). Collection, The Goldstein Foundation.*

Eugene Grigsby, **Two Girls**, *1964. Woodcut, 9 x 11" (23 x 28 cm). Courtesy of the artist.*

Bruce Onobrakpexa, **Leopard in a Cornfield**, 1965. South African. Silkscreen, 23 ¾" (60 cm) high. Collection of Frank Willett.

al-Buraq, Egyptian religious image, date unknown. Silkscreen, 22" (56 cm) in length. Courtesy Fowler Museum of Cultural History, UCLA.

Betty LaDuke, **African Water Carriers**, 1987. Etching, 22 x 30" (56 x 76 cm). Photograph: Douglas Campbell-Smith.

Katsushika Hokusai, **The Kirifuri Waterfall at Mt. Kurokami, Shimozuke Province**, *late eighteenth century. Woodcut, 14⅝ x 9⅝" (37 x 24 cm). Collection, William Rockhill Nelson Gallery of Art, Atkins Museum of Fine Arts, Kansas City, Missouri.*

Torii Kiyotada, **An Actor of the Ichikawa Clan in a Dance Movement**, *ca. 1715. Woodcut, 11¼ x 6" (29 x 15 cm). The Metropolitan Museum of Art, Harris Brisbane Dick Fund 1949.*

Trieu Au, on Her Elephant, Leads a Vietnamese Army Against Invading Chinese in A.D. 248. *Print, Vietnamese, date unknown. Courtesy Maurice Durand Collection of Vietnamese Art, Yale University Library.*

glossary

artist's proof One of a small group of prints set aside from an edition for the artist's use.

Arkansas stone A hard stone used with oil to sharpen steel tools for wood and linoleum cuts and intaglio plate development.

baren A Japanese tool for applying pressure to the back of the print-making paper while making a wood-cut. It is made of a round, flat disk covered with a bamboo leaf.

bench hook In relief printing, a device used to hold a wood block in place on a table while carving it.

bevel To file the edge of a print-making plate. The plate is filed at a forty-five degree angle to prevent it from tearing the printmaking paper and felts during printing on an etching press.

binder A substance that holds the particles of pigment together in an ink or paint.

blanket Wool felts, usually three, used on an etching press to apply a cushioned pressure to the paper during printing.

bleed print A print in which the image exceeds the edge of the paper on one or more sides.

bleeding The movement of ink beyond the edges of the printing plate. Usually caused by too much ink on the plate or too much pressure.

blockout Any material applied to a plate, block or screen to prevent a specific area from printing.

blotter Absorbent paper used to remove excess moisture from print-making paper prior to printing.

body The density or viscosity of an ink.

bon à tirer proof The "right to print" proof, designated by the artist as the standard against which every print in the edition will be judged.

brayer A hard rubber roller with a handle used to apply ink to a surface. It may also be used as a baren under certain circumstances.

burnisher In relief printing, any device used to push the paper against the inked surface in order to pick up the ink and make a print.

burnt plate oil Raw linseed oil that has been ignited to burn off lighter oils contained in it. This thick oil is added to printing ink to make it more viscous.

calcium carbonate ($CaCO_3$) An alkaline material added to papermaking fibers before they are made into sheets. It acts as a residual buffer to counteract any acidic condition that the paper might encounter.

cardboard relief print A print made in the relief manner from inked pieces of corrugated cardboard or mat board that are attached to a base before printing.

charge To cover the silk screen with ink prior to printing.

chine collé A technique for gluing smaller pieces of paper onto a print while you are printing it. Usually thin papers are attached to a heavier printing paper with this method. Historically used to tone areas in a print.

chop mark An image pressed into the print to identify the printmaking studio or the artist. Usually it is a small embossing on a lower corner of the paper.

collagraph A print made from a plate composed of other materials — papers, fabric, lace, gesso — that are often glued to a support material such as dense cardboard, masonite or Plexiglas.

composite print A print made from a number of individual plates combining different techniques or images in the same print.

cotton linter Cotton fiber available in pre-processed sheets to the hand papermaker.

couching (pronounced COO-ching) The process of transferring a wet, newly-made sheet of paper off the papermaking screen onto a paper-maker's felt in order to press it to remove excess water before the paper is dried.

counterproof A print taken from another newly-made print rather than from a plate. The counter-proof looks exactly like the image on the printmaking plate, unlike the print, which is reversed.

dauber A small, hand-held roll of felt used for spreading ink onto an intaglio plate.

deckle A wooden frame that sits on top of the papermaking screen. It holds the wet pulp in place while the sheet is being formed. Also a term for the naturally ragged edge on a handmade sheet of paper.

dimensional stability The quality of a printmaking paper, determined by how much it shrinks or stretches under the pressure of the printmaking process.

documentation sheet A form that describes the events related to the printing of a specific image, the techniques used, the size of the edition, the size of the image, the size and type of paper used, the number of artist's proofs, the inks used, where it was printed and by whom.

edition A set of identical prints, numbered and signed by the artist.

embossed print A relief or intaglio print in which the image appears raised from the surface of the paper.

end grain The side of a block of wood that does not show the grain of the wood. This surface is used in wood engravings.

engraving A technique in which an image is produced by cutting into a plate with a tool. This image is printed by forcing ink into the lines that have been cut and then printing under heavy pressure.

etching An intaglio printmaking technique in which a metal plate is first covered with an acid-resistant ground, then worked with an etching needle to create an image. The metal exposed by the needle is then "eaten into" by acid in a bath. The acid creates depressed lines in the plate which is then cleaned, inked and printed under heavy pressure.

etching press An intaglio printing press consisting of two large rollers and a sliding bedplate, usually made of metal. The bottom roller supports the bedplate on which the inked plate and paper are placed. They are then covered with three layers of felt blankets. The top roller is turned by a handle and presses the paper against the plate to create the print.

foxing Brown stains on paper produced by the oxidation of iron particles in the paper.

gesso A mixture of gypsum and glue useful in collagraph printmaking to create texture and line.

ghost image In monotype printmaking, the second image pulled from a printmaking plate.

gouge In relief printmaking, a broad tool used for clearing away non-image areas from the wood or linoleum block.

grain In wood, the direction in which the transportation tissue of the tree grows, normally thought of as the length of the board.

halo An oil stain sometimes found around a color in a print produced with oil-based ink. Sometimes referred to as a butter stain.

Hollander Beater The traditional European machine for processing rags into paper pulp. A circular drum fitted with metal blades macerates the fibers while mixing them with water.

hot pressed paper A smooth surface produced on paper by running it through a series of heated metal rollers.

impasto On a print, a raised area produced by a heavy buildup of ink.

ink Pigment combined with a binder.

intaglio (pronounced "in-TAHL-ee-oh") Printing techniques in which paper is pushed into inked depressions in the printmaking plate in order to create the image. Etching, mezzotint, engraving, aquatint, drypoint and collagraph are intaglio techniques.

kozo The Japanese fiber most often used for printmaking papers.

laid line On a papermaking mold, the metal rods that form the screen on which the paper is formed. On paper, the image created by these metal rods.

light-fastness The ability of a paper, ink, dye or paint to withstand exposure to light without changing color.

linoleum print A relief print made by cutting into linoleum.

lithography A planographic technique in which the image area on the lithograph stone or metal plate is treated chemically to accept ink and the non-image area is treated to repel ink.

moldmade paper Machine-made paper.

monoprint A print pulled from an etching, woodblock or collagraph plate that has been altered, making it unique. For example, in the case of an edition of etchings printed in

black, printing one in red ink would make it a monoprint.

monotype A print pulled in an edition of one from a painted plate that has no permanent markings on it, usually Plexiglas, glass or metal.

pigment Coloring material in ink or paint. Can be from natural sources or synthetically made.

plank side The side of a piece of wood on which a woodcut is made. Referred to as the grain side as opposed to the end grain side.

plate mark The imprint into the sheet of paper caused by the thickness of the printing plate during intaglio printing.

plate tone Areas of color on the print caused by a thin film of ink left on the plate after an image is pulled. This can be accidental or intentional.

pochoir (pronounced "POE-schwahr") A printmaking technique involving a stencil used to print small areas of color.

print An image produced by placing paper, cloth or other materials in contact with an inked surface and applying pressure, or by pressing ink onto a surface through a stencil.

proof print A trial print pulled to test technical aspects of an image.

pull To print an image.

pulp The basic ingredient of paper in its wet stage.

quire Twenty-four sheets of paper.

ream Five hundred sheets of paper.

reduction block print A relief print made by alternately cutting and printing the same block, usually working from light colors to dark colors.

registration marks Marks made on the press bedplate or on the printing surface to help insure that the paper is in exactly the same position every time it is run through the press or otherwise printed.

relief printing Printmaking techniques in which the image is printed from the raised areas of the printmaking block. These are usually created by cutting away areas of the block. Wood and linoleum as well as collagraph prints are considered relief prints.

rice paper A term sometimes applied to all Oriental style papers.

serigraphy Printing techniques that make use of a flat tool to force ink through a stencil directly onto paper. Also called silkscreen printing.

silkscreen printing See *serigraphy*.

sizing A substance added during or after the papermaking process to reduce the absorbency of the paper.

solvent A substance used for dissolving another substance. Oil-based inks are dissolved in turpentine, kerosene and other organic solvents. Water-based inks are solvent in water.

squeegee A silkscreen tool used for pushing ink through a stencil onto paper or fabric. It consists of a blade made of rubber, polyurethane or plastic mounted in a wooden handle.

suite A related group of original prints.

tarlatan Sheer cotton fabric, heavily sized and used to wipe ink from a plate.

veiner Small U- or V-shaped gouges used for wood block cutting.

water leaf paper Unsized paper.

wood engraving A relief print made on the end grain of a block of wood.

wood pulp paper Paper made from cellulose wood fibers, often buffered to reduce its acidity.

woodcut A relief print made on the plank side of a block of wood.

wove screen A screen for hand or machine-made papers composed of fine brass wires woven to produce a smooth, even paper.

suppliers

General Supplies

Daniel Smith, Artists' Materials
4130 First Avenue South
Seattle, WA 98134-2302

Graphic Chemical and Ink Co.
P.O. Box 27
728 North Yale Avenue
Villa Park, IL 60181

New York Central Art Supply
62 Third Avenue
New York, NY 10003

Handschy Chemical Company
528 North Fulton Street
Indianapolis, IN 46202

Rembrandt Graphic Arts Company
P.O. Box 130
Rosemont, NJ 08556

The Craftool Company
1 Industrial Road
Woodbridge, NJ 07075

Aiko's Art Materials
3347 North Clark Street
Chicago, IL 60657

T.W. Graphics Group
7220 East Slauson Avenue
City of Commerce, CA 90040

Presses

American French Tool Company
P.O. Box 227
Coventry, RI 02816

Charles Brand Press
84 East 19th Street
New York, NY 10003

Conrad Machine Co.
1525 South Warner
Whitehall, MI 49461

Dickerson Press Company
P.O. Box 8
South Haven, MI 49090

KB Press
Applied Arts International
22313 Meekland Avenue
Hayward, CA 94541

Bunch Presses
2456 Springrose Circle
Verona, WI 53593

Printing Blankets

Continental Felt Company
22 West 15th Street
New York, NY 10011

Ink

Charbonnel
13 Quai Montebello
Paris, France

Hunt Manufacturing Company
230 South Broad Street
Philadelphia, PA 19102-4167

Naz-Dar Company
1087 North Branch Street
Chicago, IL 60622

Papers

Twinrocker Paper Company
P.O. Box 413
Brookston, IN 47923

Dieu Donne Papermill
3 Crosby Street
New York, NY 10013

Rugg Road Paper and Prints
1 Fitchburg Street, #B154
Somerville, MA 02143

bibliography

Brommer, Gerald F., *Relief Printmaking*. Worcester, MA: Davis Publications, Inc., 1970.

Chamberlain, Walter, *Manual of Woodcut Printmaking*. New York: Charles Scribner's Sons, 1978.

Clapp, Anne F., *Curatorial Care of Works of Art on Paper*. New York: Lyons and Burford Publishers, 1987.

Clark, Nancy, Thomas Cutter, and Jean-Ann McGrane, *Ventilation: A Practical Guide*. New York: Center for Safety in the Arts, 1984.

Heller, Jules, *Printmaking Today*. New York: Holt, Rinehart and Winston, 1958.

Langdale, Cecily, *Monotypes by Maurice Prendergast*. Chicago: Terra Museum of American Art, 1984.

Leaf, Ruth, *Intaglio Printmaking Techniques*. New York: Watson-Guptill Publications, 1976.

McCann, Michael, *Health Hazards Manual for Artists*. New York: Lyons and Burford Publishers, 1985.

Peterdi, Gabor, *Printmaking Methods Old and New*. New York: Macmillan and Sons, 1971.

Rasmusen, Henry, *Printmaking with Monotype*. Philadelphia, PA: Chilton Book Company, 1960.

Saff, Donald and Deli Sacilotto, *Printmaking: History and Process*. New York: Holt, Rinehart and Winston, 1978.

The Painterly Print, New York: Metropolitan Museum of Art, 1980.

index